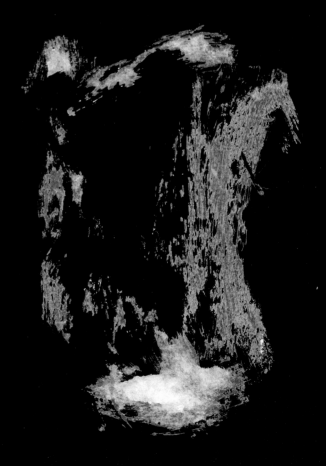

# GRAND HOTEL

## THE GOLDEN AGE OF PALACE HOTELS

## AN ARCHITECTURAL AND SOCIAL HISTORY

INTRODUCTION

JEAN D'ORMESSON

of the Académie Française

◆

TEXTS

DAVID WATKIN
HUGH MONTGOMERY-MASSINGBERD
PIERRE-JEAN RÉMY
FRÉDÉRIC GRENDEL

◆

CONCEPTION & DESIGN

MARC WALTER

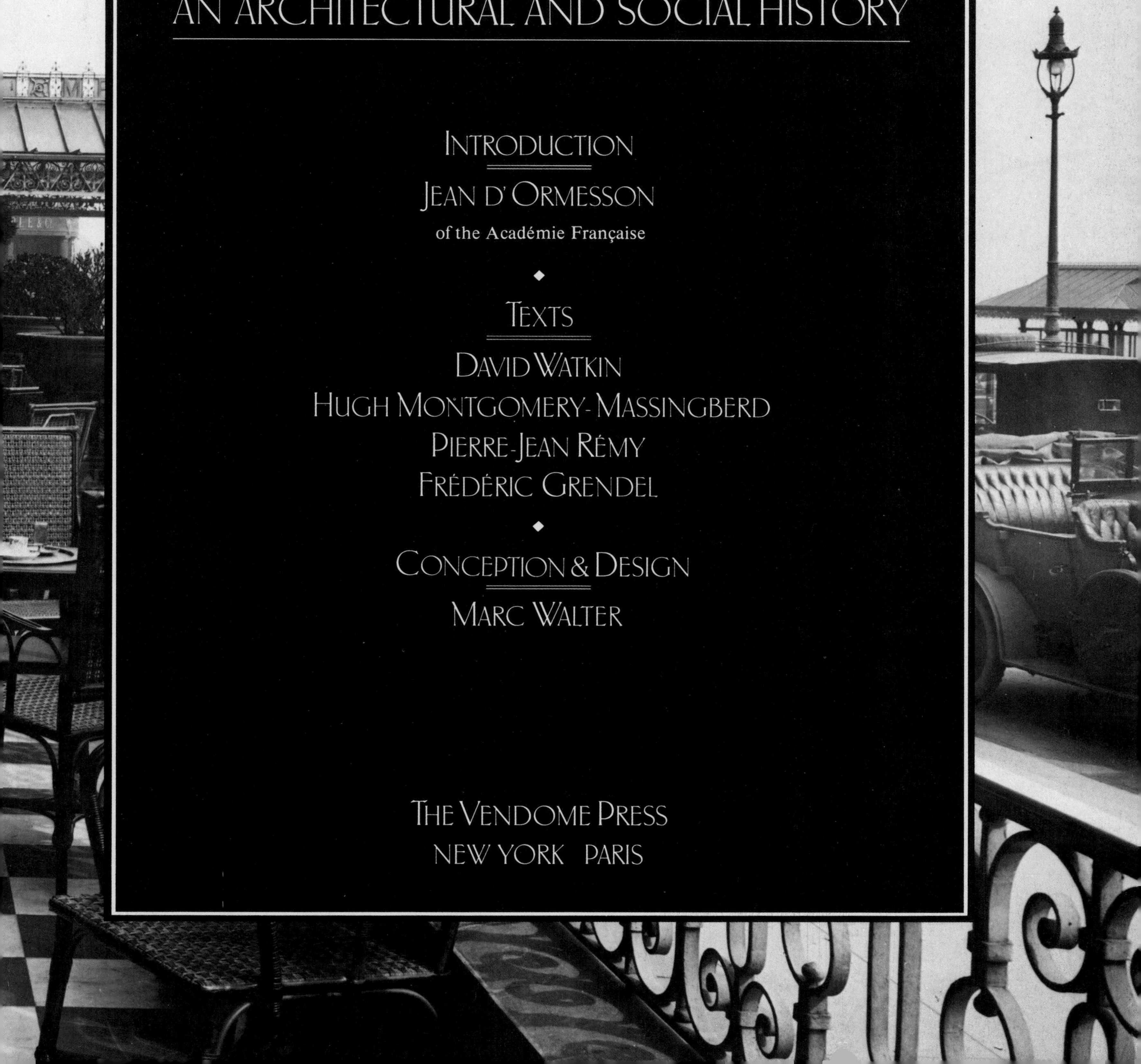

THE VENDOME PRESS

NEW YORK   PARIS

———————ACKNOWLEDGEMENTS———————

We would like to thank the hotels who have
allowed documents from their archives to be
reproduced.
    We would also like to thank the many people who
have helped us in the preparation of this book
including: Mr Aletti, Mr and Mrs Balaudo, Mr
Barnier, Miss Begeja, Mr Boissel, Mr F. X. Bouchart,
Mr Bresler, Mr Carle, Mrs Debuisson, Mr Hansen,
Mrs Krainick Negresco, Mr Mangin, Mr Marrey,
Mr Nappier, Mr Helmut Newton, Mr Roche, Mr
Rudovsky, Mr Salvadori, Mr Savine, Mr J. N. de Soye,
Mr Taittinger, Mr Van Dam, Mr Weil.

First published in 1984 in Great Britain by
J. M. Dent and Sons Ltd., London

© 1984 by The Vendome Press, New York and Marc Walter, Paris

Published in the U.S.A. by
The Vendome Press
515 Madison Avenue, New York City 10022

Distributed in the U.S.A. by
The Viking Press
40 West 23rd Street, New York City 10010

Distributed in Canada by Methuen Publications

Picture research by Noëlle Gauthier
Captions by Catherine Donzel and Marc Walter
Translated from the French by
Daniel K. Wheeler, Martine Meade and Murray Wyllie

Designed and produced by Marc Walter

**Library of Congress Cataloging in Publication Data**
Main entry under title:

The Golden age of palace hotels.

1. Hotels, taverns, etc.--Europe--History--19th century
--Addresses, essays, lectures. 2. Hotels, taverns, etc.
--Europe--History--20th century-- Addresses, essays,
lectures. 3. Hotels, taverns, etc.  -- United States--
History -- 19th century -- Addresses,  essays, lectures.
4. Hotels, taverns, etc. --United States--History--20th
century--Addresses, essays, lectures. I. Watkin, David,
1941–
    NA7850.E85G6  1984  940.2'8  84-7299
        ISBN 0-86565-040-3

Printed and bound in Hong Kong
by Mandarin Offset Ltd.

# TABLE OF CONTENTS

*Previous pages:*
*Staff at the* Hotel Excelsior, *Berlin.*
Metropole Hotel, *Brighton.*
*Banquet at the* Hôtel Meurice, *Paris.*

# INTRODUCTION

## JEAN D'ORMESSON

To speak of grand hotels is to speak of shades of yesteryear, of shrines to another era, of legendary havens for exotic travellers and exiles rich as Croesus, of ephemeral abodes for hedonists in pursuit of luxury and heavenly bliss, or, if you will, of the romance between wealth and poetry, of dwellings where sheer splendour carries the day in a frenzied modern world.

*The interior of a deluxe train in 1912: the restaurant car.*

There would be no such thing as grand hotels if people did not travel. The ancestor of all wanderers is, of course, Ulysses, wily navigator and pioneer investigator of travel's thousand subtle charms. Only a sybarite such as he could have survived the myriad misfortunes that befell this son of Laertes, who in the teeth of divine wrath remained the focus of an epic that has come down through the ages in the form of myth. Ulysses is the traveller's archetype, the very model of all those who linger on their way hither and yon, who in their fascination with worldly marvels are forever reluctant to go home. He is the symbol of the roving escapist, without whom there would be no way stations, no inns, *pensiones*, or hotels, certainly no magnificent ones, those that behold the sea, that invite one to dally, those whose architecture mirrors that of palaces fit for Kings and Fairy Queens.

Having spoken of these glorious establishments, we require little imagination to recall the legendary figures of our own era : Don Quixote, for whom the lowliest hovel would turn into a sumptuous abode ; the aged Faust in quest of his youth ; not to mention Don Juan, tirelessly pursuing the fleeting silhouettes of chambermaids and young Marquises, eternal rivals set in formal French gardens or beneath the gilded panelling of Rococo drawing rooms. Could it be that the Devil himself inhabits these great *caravanseraglios*, where temptation and luxury go hand in hand ?

Sooner or later, every hero of literature must turn up in one of our planet's grand hotels. The characters of Le Sage, the Abbé Prévost, Chateaubriand, Stendhal, Proust, and Musset have been immortalized as they make their way down those corridors and stairways. Many of them continue to haunt the lofty rooms of the Danieli overlooking the world's most spectacular urban setting. I might add that this paean to the divinity of grand hotels should not come from me, but from my master, Paul Morand. The latter would show up in a fast open car, either alone or in the company of a young woman, spend a single night at best, question everybody in sight, from the valets to the *demi-mondaines* ; then, in a matter of mere weeks, he would bring forth, to much acclaim, one of his books, each a breathless exposé of modern life's throbbing tempo.

Books are not alone in fanning the flames of our love for grand hotels. Gastronomy, politics, music, romance, and, last but not least, the world of money — all feed the legend too. Millionaire Barnabooth, a character born of novelist Larbaud's sorrowful whimsy, lived full time in the grandest of grand hotels, far from his native Vichy, dividing his days between the joys of literature and money. Unlike Morand, Barnabooth did not do his travelling in a bright red Italian roadster, nor in an austere British job. Instead, he would alight from the Orient Express laden with the leather suitcases he would immediately hurl from the very bridges of his lavish lifestyle and disillusionment. Nothing was too good for him, nor too expensive or too grand. Barnabooth was the grand hotel's ideal guest, for he was rich and meant to make his dreams come true.

There is absolutely no denying that life in grand hotels requires not only money but imagination as well. We all know the part played in the world of these establishments by Swiss hotel schools, Italian opera, French taste, British tradition, the German mark, and the Yankee dollar. But something more is needed in order for an hotel to become truly grand, something other than just another comfortable place to stay, with well-appointed bathrooms and impersonal bedrooms. And that something is fantasy. However much it may be a tool of the tourist trade, a pleasant place to meet people, a familiar address, a feather in a country's cap, and an asset in the international balance of trade, a grand hotel is, above all else, a Pandora's box of sweet dreams.

If it is to be worthy of the name, a grand hotel must distinguish itself from those anonymous establishments meant to make the travelling American feel at home. Not that Hiltons and Holiday Inns, or France's Sofitels and Italy's Jollys are to be disdained. At the end of many a rough if exhilarating journey without electricity or running water, I have been happy enough to land in a Hilton Hotel at, say, Teheran or Athens, with their identical architecture and interchangeable local colour. I have leapt for joy in Parma to discover an hotel with the wonderfully apt name of Jolly-Stendhal. Still, no true grand hotel can be part of a chain. There may well be links and similarities, just as there are, for instance, Ritz Hotels everywhere. Simply because the name appealed to me, I have even made the mistake of staying at a Ritz Hotel in India, even though the Taj Mahal Hotel was silently beckoning me. The fact is that these namesakes are not all created alike, and, as with the wheat and the chaff, a notable difference obtains between the Ritz Hotels in Paris, London, and Madrid and some of their cousins. As in many other things — women, Kings, romances, and, for that matter, people's lives — comparisons are useless when it comes to grand hotels, however many there may be. It will not do to compare the Hôtel des Trois Rois in Basel to the Lausanne Palace, or the Beverly Hills Hotel with the Eden Roc. Uniformity is by definition alien to grand hotels, for they are invariably unique.

The grand hotel is unique first of all because of its location — always on the seashore, overlooking a lake, on top of a mountain, or in the heart of an historic city. Moreover, its architecture makes the grand hotel a one-of-a-kind phenomenon. An ugly grand hotel is quite simply a contradiction in terms, unless the ugliness has become a legend in its own right and thus transcended the very notion of beauty, as has been the case with some women who, despite a reputation for plainness, succeed in making themselves irresistible.

> Women call the lady an armadillo
> But men go mad with her tease
> While the Archbishop of Toledo
> Sings Mass down on his knees.

And last, but not least, the grand hotel gains uniqueness from its charm, history, and legends, not to mention that certain aura so characteristic of all things beautiful, whether they be *femmes fatales* or international grand hotels.

Every grand hotel has its legend, and that is what makes its heart beat and gives the place its identity. No wonder an hotel attains the coveted status of grand only with difficulty. It takes a grand hotel for a legend to arise, but no hotel is grand without a legend, making a vicious circle that can be broken only by the truly great. The legends on which grand hotels thrive belong to the arena of history and literature, to be sure, but also to the world of the theatre and films, of music, opera, sports, horse races, the stock market, industry, and to the vestiges of Atlantis, that vanished continent formerly known as *society*. Snobbery, needless to say, is no stranger to the world of grand hotels.

Not only snobbery, we might add, but also vice, theft, and crime, and they are all linked in some unspoken, ambiguous way. It does not hurt a grand hotel, for instance, to have been the scene of a scandal. Of course, such things should not be overdone, and never would I suggest that a grand hotel cultivate the reputation of a brigands' lair likely to relieve prominent guests of their wallets, jewels, and, on occasion, their very lives. Still, an infinitesimally small, medicinal dose of suicides and high, romantic passion may come in good stead, for fascination and snobbery flourish as much on misfortune as they do on bliss, provided both assume grandiose proportions, as behooves a grand hotel.

I have known some wonderful hotels, have been in love with a few inns, and had a delectable time in the odd *pension de famille*. Bahia, Venice, Montepulciano, Cuernavaca, the area southwest of Mont-de-Marsan, all of Switzerland and Austria, the romantic, merciless reaches of southern Germany, Provence, Dalmatia, the Greek islands and the area round Granada, the Amalfi coast and my beloved Apulia — all are places where I have left behind as many memories as I could have garnered in a thousand years of travel. Most arise from tiny rooms tucked away

Hall and lounge in the
Hôtel Ruhl, *Nice*.

in equally tiny establishments, one of whose main appeals lies in the touchingly small number of keys dangling from the board behind the reception desk — twenty at the most, sometimes no more than five or six. No one has said it better than J.P. Toulet in his modest hymn to down-and-out travellers, penniless students, and poor lovers locked in tight embrace under the flowering wistaria :

> Do you remember the little inn
> And all my gallantry that day ?
> You wore a dress of white piqué,
> As pure as the Blessed Virgin.
>
> Then came a Navarese vagrant
> To serenade us with his guitar.
> How I adored our life in Navarre,
> Love too, and cool wine to decant.
>
> For the sweet auberge in the Landes
> I long — and would like to remark
> The hostess with her kerchief so dark,
> Swagged in wistaria garlands.

Alas, such topics as young love and *oaristys* are not the subject of this book. The matter at hand is considerably less innocent, less guileless, and, at any rate, less pure : a world of extravagance and burning passion, whose chronicler is not Toulet but Richard Wagner. Here, we are not cavorting among shepherdesses, but among *monstres sacrés* and captains of industry ; not among young lovers, to the sweet sound of bucolic flutes, but in a world full of *Sturm und Drang*, to the thunder of organ music. We drink champagne as if there were no tomorrow, and we move through a universe where bloodshed, bankruptcy, folly, and frenzy form the order of the day. We have entered the world of Orson Welles's *Citizen Kane*, of Luchino Visconti's ancient and decadent families.

Hardly have you pulled up at the door when you are swept along by the trappings of this flamboyant realm. A giant in a doorman's uniform opens the door of your automobile and, if necessary, protects you from the rain with an outsized red umbrella, thereby ushering you into that holy of holies, the main lobby. The place is lit up by a blaze of glittering lights, and you could hear a pin drop. A grand hotel's main lobby could scarcely be more antithetical to that of a railway station. Whereas the latter fairly vibrates with the hustle and bustle of people on their way somewhere, the former radiates the calm of people who have arrived and thus live in hushed composure. They find rugs under their feet, antiquated armchairs, a bar where the only soul to be seen is the perennial alcoholic — the only person in the entire place to know a few lines of verse, which he will recite before downing his drink and casually breaking his glass — a small rickety lift fitted in next to the monumental staircase for invalids and guests in their nineties and, last but not least, the main protagonist in the local mythology, a veritable figure out of a Greek tragedy, the man with the golden keys, who acts as a middleman between the rich in need and the powerful in distress : the concierge.

Bellhops, waiters, captains, wine stewards, chambermaids, masseurs, cloakroom attendants, house detectives, handymen, plumbers, electricians, barmen, and the usual bevy of cosmopolitan young women — all play second fiddle to the concierge, the central figure of this dubious no man's land, where both fringes of a pleasure-seeking world come to rub shoulders : hirelings, male and female, the privileged few, so-called scum, and those who pass for 'upright', an occasional synonym for rich. A whole comedy of manners is staged round the concierge, who is no stranger to the darkest recesses of anyone's heart and acts as a one-man chorus to the entire tragicomedy. Perched atop his observatory, he presides over the follies and the aberrations of the mighty. In the old days there used to be the grand old man of Venice, the concierge ensconced on his throne at the Bauer-Grünwald, a stone's throw from San Moisé's elaborate Baroque façade, halfway between those two institutions, the Danieli Hotel and the Gritti Palace, long before the Cipriani had begun to lure American millionaires off to the frontier of the civilized world, out towards San Giorgio and La Giudecca. He could get you theatre tickets when the Fenice was sold out, and plane tickets for Paris, New York, or London even though all seats had been booked on Air France and Alitalia.

Diminutive but dauntless, this concierge — whose name, Tortorella, meant dove — wielded more power than the Mayor, the Cardinal, and all the descendants of Popes and Doges combined. In the world of Venice's grand hotels, Tortorella played the part of both the angel Heurtebise and of Asmodeus, king demons.

Édouard Bourdet has immortalized yet another prominent figure from the realm of grand hotels, the captain of the Ritz Hotel on the Place Vendôme, to whom he gave the name Olivier. Olivier was the confidant of South American beauties on the wane, a providential source of funds and sound advice to young blades, and the confessor of international financiers, who also made good use of his infallible psychological insights. In this rootless world, he stood for common sense and compassion, a living example of the fact that, whatever else might be said about concierges and captains and their more or less legitimate activities, these figures do bring a humane touch to the glossy atmosphere of grand hotels.

Different though they may be, grand hotels as a category constitute a sort of microcosm set apart from the rest of the planet. It is possible to circle the globe by going from one grand hotel to another, in the same way that people nowadays go airport-hopping. Taking off from Paris or London, one can be at the Alhambra in Granada in a matter of hours, at the Mamounia in Marrakech, or at Cap d'Antibes's celebrated Eden Roc. Some of these hotels bask in fame, while others are as demure as young girls ready to blush at the mere thought of attracting attention. The Palace at St. Moritz, the Sacher and the Schwarzenberg in Vienna, the Hassler and the Excelsior in Rome, the Waldorf-Astoria in New York are world-renowned. Meanwhile, the Fuschl near Salzburg would be virtually unknown had it not served as a setting for Romy Schneider in the role of Sissi. But whether glamorous or inconspicuous, the most enthralling grand hotels on earth are those that boast a history, a legend, a hinterland of memories and myths which have dimly survived the harsh realities of today's world. No one has been more articulate on that subject than Somerset Maugham when he wrote of the illustrious Raffles Hotel in Singapore : 'It stands for all the fables of the exotic East'. That particular sentence was enough to set me prowling through virtually empty lobbies and into seedy lounges full of elderly English ladies sipping cups of bitter tea. Comparable mirages will no doubt send other travellers off to different sanctuaries, however desecrated and trampled upon. In the grand hotel at Udaipur overlooking the lake, for example, the bleached-blonde wives of new-rich oilmen carry on like Maharanees. The anachronistic establishments of Baden-Baden and Marienbad are haunted by the antiquated ghosts of mediatized Princes and by the last remnants of the Austro-Hungarian monarchy that once embodied the very essence of a Central Europe long unaffected by patrician North Atlantic winds, which finally brought a merchant spirit in their wake.

No grand hotel is without its phantoms of opera singers and arms merchants. Whenever Basil Zaharoff, or Citizen Kane and his wife, any remaining English aristocrats or Italian prima donnas went anywhere, they stayed at the grand hotels portrayed in this book. These are images from another era, one that stretched from the Industrial Revolution till World War II. Before that time, most grand hotels were in fact mere inns, or else they still functioned as private homes in the hands of old aristocratic families soon forced, by the tide of history, to give them up. After that date, the grand hotels became an anachronism. As the favorite haunt of Arab Princes and official delegations, it has somehow become its own wax museum. The grand hotel's days of glory ran from the time of, say, Louis-Philippe or Napoleon III through the age of Hitler and Stalin, or if you insist, right up to May 1968. One way or another, Italian opera, heavy industry, Proust's novels, the Ballets Russes, d'Annunzio and Stavisky, world boxing championships and the 1929 Crash all have some link to grand hotels. The grand hotel as such signalled the waning of an aristocratic age during which the landed gentry never left their estates, and the onset of social decay, whose first stirrings, like those of all decay, were grandiose and full of charm. The grand hotel stands halfway between the stagecoach and nuclear power, between feudalism and concentration camps.

Verdi's *Traviata*, Strauss's waltzes, the rise of jazz, too, are symptomatic of the end of Romanticism and the birth of Surrealism, which is to say, the world of grand hotels. A *dolce far niente* transfixed by intimations of death, a taste for the gigantic that had not yet lost its elegance, a civilization that hung on for dear life in the face of doom at the hands of an incurable disease, princesses who were still Austrian, boyars who remained Russian, swarms of servants, an environment as yet unspoilt, cities that had not yet been desecrated, a shift in the conception of beauty and morality that was a corollary to the rise of oil and the dollar and to the all-pervasive fact of politics ; a tiny handful of slightly jaded, privileged people on the one hand, multitudes banging at the gates on the other — all that as well went hand in hand with the phenomenon of grand hotels. *Que la fête commence !* as the phrase went, but, alas, barely had the party begun when it was already coming to an end.

Let us now make our way through revolving doors framed by heavy columns, and enter a main lobby where the concierge will sit majestically enthroned behind the reception desk. Over here will be the perennial English nobleman flanked by two unattached young women. Over there will be the vast dining room with its dozen waiters hovering over some five or six guests. Do not miss the chandeliers, the staircase, the antique wood panelling, or the tapestries. Look round the bedchambers and royal suites with their sitting rooms, their sparkling new pink or blue tiled bathrooms, outsized bathtubs, and swan-shaped faucets, and do not forget to take in the view of the city, the lake, the countryside, or the sea. What you are about to behold is the fanciful world of grand hotels, the grand hotels of our dreams.

*Arriving at Vichy station.*

# THE GRAND HOTEL STYLE

## DAVID WATKIN

The grand hotel and the railway station, institutions frequently linked in the first half of the nineteenth century, were perhaps the two most striking new building types to emerge in the Victorian era. The development of easy and rapid transport altered people's social expectations, while the accompanying grand hotel also fostered a new detachment from ancient patterns of living. Overnight accommodation in the course of travelling ceased to be a painful necessity and became an occasion to indulge in a fantasy world where travellers could imagine themselves liberated from the responsibilities of the family and the private house. It is this romantic escapism that, in part, accounts for the continuing popular fascination with grand hotels felt even in our own day. The hotel constitutes a kind of theatre in which visitors act out a life that may have little relation to their experience in the real world outside.

Conventional histories of Western architecture concentrate up to the mid-eighteenth century on two building types : the church and the palace. Thereafter the types increase rapidly, but several of them — the opera house or theatre, the library and the museum — were in fact attributes of the palace expanded to cater for a prosperous middle class. When Charles Garnier designed the staircase hall for the Paris Opéra (1861-1874) he not only made it more sumptuous than any outside a royal palace, but also quite deliberately envisaged it as a setting for an elaborate social ritual as spectacular as anything likely to take place on the stage. For Garnier, indeed, the spectators themselves were actors. This larger-than-life element, a fundamental part of the appeal of the opera house and the grand hotel, is also present in another characteristically nineteenth-century building type : the club. The London clubs were supposedly built in a way to provide their members with some of the comforts they enjoyed in their private houses. However, the only houses the clubs resembled were the town palaces of millionaire Whig noblemen ; thus, an element of fantasy prevailed in the design of clubs used by the higher or even the highest reaches of society. In the nineteenth century, when the Kings and Princes retained much of their feudal power, it was still no act of fantasy to build real palaces, and many of those erected by European royalty were no less magnificent than the grandest of grand hotels. But with the collapse of so many monarchies in the twentieth century came the virtual disappearance of the large-scale royal palace as a building type, leaving the grand hotel to assume an even more suggestive role as the heir to an otherwise vanished world.

Interestingly enough, it was democratic America, entirely lacking in royal palaces, that first developed the grand hotel. The earliest major American hotel was the City Hotel in

Hotel Bayerischer Hof, *Munich.*
*Left page:* Waldorf Hotel, *New York.*

New York, erected in 1794-1796 with seventy-three rooms on five floors. The City Hotel still belonged to the tradition of the European inn, but within a year Benjamin Henry Latrobe (1764-1820), the brilliant English-born architect who became the father of nineteenth-century classical architecture in America, had drawn up plans for what would have given Richmond, Virginia, and history their first giant hotel. Conceived as the flanking wing of a group with a theatre at the centre and assembly rooms on the other side, the Latrobe project was clearly foreseen as part of a new social way of life.

An hotel approaching the scale of Latrobe's was actually built in Boston in 1806-1809, from designs by the city's leading architect, Asher Benjamin. The fact that it would be called the Exchange Coffee House reflects the unfamiliarity of the building type. However, with 7 storeys and 200 apartments, a dining room for 300, a domed ballroom, a subscription library, and a Masonic Hall, the new hostelry gave Boston more a social centre than either a coffee house or an hotel. Meanwhile, Latrobe's visionary scheme, which had come close to an exercise in town planning, was finally realized at Baden-Baden, Germany, in 1807-1809 by the architect and town-planner Friedrich Weinbrenner (1766-1826). Under Weinbrenner's guidance, Karlsruhe from 1800-1825 became the model for the post-Napoleonic transformation of German royal-residence towns into nineteenth-century cities dominated by major civic buildings. The hotel that Weinbrenner built at Baden-Baden, the Badischer Hof, was a novel social complex that, significantly enough, the architect created by converting the buildings of a former Capuchin convent. In his noble design for the hotel dining room, with its flanking rows of giant columns, Weinbrenner seemed to imply that in Catholic Baden-Baden a secular building could be as magnificent as an ecclesiastical one. The Badischer Hof also boasted a ballroom with a movable stage, a library and reading room, sitting rooms, 48 bedrooms, 11 water closets, extensive stables, and a bathing establishment. To those visiting Baden-Baden, which was about to enter a boom period as one of the nineteenth century's most successful spa towns, it must have seemed as though the great baths of ancient Rome had been transported to Germany and made residential.

In England, John Foulston (1772-1842) designed a similarly revolutionary building, the Royal Hotel Assembly Rooms and Theatre erected at Plymouth, Devon, in 1811-1822. Foulston was to rebuild Plymouth as a model Neoclassical town somewhat in the way Weinbrenner, on a larger

*Drawing room in a suite at the* Grosvenor Hotel, *London.*

scale, had rebuilt Karlsruhe, though his provision of a theatre echoes Latrobe rather than Weinbrenner. Constructed round a large courtyard, the Royal contained a theatre and a ballroom, fifty bedrooms, stables, and a coach house. Next to it Foulston built the Athenaeum (1818-1819) as the premises of the Plymouth literary and philosophical society.

The imposing seventeen-bay façade of the Royal complex, with its monumental eight-column Ionic portico, cannot have looked like anyone's idea of an hotel at that time. Nonetheless, Foulston's coldly grand Neoclassical façade, if not his combination of hotel and theatre, became the norm in Europe and North America for large early-nineteenth-century hotels, among them the Regent Hotel (1819) at Leamington Spa, Warwickshire, by Charles Harriott Smith (1792-1864), the even more imposing Queen's Hotel (1836-1838) at Cheltenham, by R.W. Jearrad, the Royal Western Hotel (1837-1839) at Bristol by R.S. Pope, and Tremont House (1828-1829 ; demolished in 1894) at Boston, designed by Isaiah Rogers to replace the Exchange Coffee House, which had burnt down in 1818. Like the English hotels just mentioned, the Tremont was a monumental pile with a sober classical mien. Clad in white Quincy granite, it did not look sumptuous or frivolous but eminently respectable, like a courthouse, academy, or athenaeum. In fact, it was also not unlike the Ducal Palace at Wiesbaden, built in 1835-1837 by Georg Moller from a plan that adapted itself to a corner site in a similarly clever way.

Tremont House, the first modern hotel in America, did not obscure its function by providing ballrooms, assembly rooms, or theatres. It was simply a first-class hotel that, with 170 rooms and a dining room capable of seating 200, reigned as the largest in the world, offering French cuisine and aiming exclusively for the top and richest stratum of European and American visitors. The novel plan, marked by its domed central lobby and lateral corridor, its distinction between single and double rooms, its numerous handsomely furnished public rooms, its complete isolation of the stables, and its lack of a signboard outside the front entrance, made a deliberate and total break with the traditional travellers' inn. Novel, too, were the Tremont's mechanical and other services, which included eight baths with cold running water in the basement and a row of eight water closets on the ground floor, gas light in the public rooms, and a different key for all the bedrooms, each of them provided with free soap, an unusual extravagance at that date.

At Tremont House a new building type was born. The hotel immediately became one of the sights of Boston, and in response to public demand, William H. Eliot wrote a monograph on it. Published in 1830 under the title *A Description of Tremont House, with Architectural Illustrations*, the book remained a manual for hotel design for half a century. One feature that linked Tremont House with the City Hotel in New York and Boston's Exchange Coffee House was that all three had been financed by stock companies. The hotel built by a corporation as part of a programme of commercial investment was a new phenomenon, one that would become an essential ingredient of the promotion of grand hotels in both the United States and Europe. The rapid expansion of America, the great distances between towns and the lack of traditional patterns all encouraged the growth of hotels. Every town in the burgeoning new country eagerly sought to have its own Tremont House as a symbol of success and popularity. The first serious rival to the Boston institution came with Astor House (1832-1836) in New York, nearly twice the Tremont's size and promoted by the first American to amass a great fortune, John Jacob Astor. This, too, was designed by Isaiah Rogers, who performed the same service for Burnet House (1850) in Cincinnati. Similar hotels were Henry Whitestone's second Galt House at Louisville in Midwestern America. The South, meanwhile, saw the arrival of George Purvis's second St. Charles Hotel (1850) in New Orleans and Charles Reichardt's Charleston Hotel (1839) in Charleston, South Carolina, with its spectacular Corinthian colonnade.

A rather different set of factors, including the short-lived stage-coach boom, the formation of metalled roads by Telford and Macadam, and the rise in popularity of spas and seaside resorts, encouraged the growth of large hotels in England during the 1820s and 1830s. But while the grandiose Queen's Hotel (1836-1838) in Cheltenham was a four-storey, Corinthian-porticoed pile like the second St. Charles in New Orleans, the latter had 300 bedrooms as compared to the former, which offered only about 80 bedrooms and no bathrooms or lavatories. Beginning in the 1840s, the determining factor on the development of hotels in England was the railway. In the course of that decade, hotel accommodation became an essential attribute of new railway stations. The earliest were Francis Thompson's Midland Hotel (1840) at Derby and the Victoria Station Hotel (1843) at Colchester, both of which survive in all their simplified Italianate glory. In the 1850s the success of the railway system enabled its developers to acquire sites for their stations at the centre of towns and cities rather than on their outskirts. One of the earliest of the palatial terminus hotels was the Great Western (1852-1854) at Paddington in London, designed by P.C.

Hardwick (1822-1892) in a version of the French Renaissance style. Though described at the time as 'the largest and most sumptuous hotel in England', its 150 rooms hardly made it enormous by American standards. Still, the novelty and prestige of the Great Western were such that Prince Albert visited the hotel just before its opening on 9 June 1854. It also contained a royal waiting room for the use of Queen Victoria when travelling to Windsor. The technological innovations brought to the Great Western, among them hot-water pipes in the linen cupboards, private water closets and electric clocks, prompted the *Civil Engineer and Architect's Journal* to prophesy accurately that 'the construction of such establishments has led to many ingenious appliances which will have their future place in domestic architecture'.

London gained its next mammoth luxury hotel in the seven-storey Grosvenor, built next to Victoria Station in 1860-1861 from designs by J.T. Knowles, who had devised a hybrid Italianate style with French pavilion roofs and much carved ornament composed of portrait busts as well as foliage. Soon afterwards came the 250-bedroom Charing Cross Hotel (1863-1864), designed by E.M. Barry in a similarly amorphous style but with a superb, centrally planned, domed dining hall that remains one of London's most beautiful public eating rooms.

It was no coincidence that Hardwick's Great Western Hotel at Paddington opened its doors in 1851, the year the Great Exhibition brought six million visitors to the Crystal Palace in London's Hyde Park. In 1862 the even larger International Exhibition in the Brompton Road again brought over six million visitors to the capital and provided another occasion to launch a giant hotel, the Langham, built in 1864 from designs by John Giles. Dominating Portland Place, this massive pile with its combination of Italian Gothic and French Renaissance motifs received inspection on its opening day in 1865 from 2,000 visitors, led by the Prince of Wales, whose subsequent fondness for grand hotels would do much to advance their popularity. The Langham had up to 400 beds, nearly 300 water closets, a room hopefully described as an Ambassadors' Audience Room, two libraries, a much-prized hydraulic lift, of a type Elisha Otis had pioneered eight years before in New York, and a courtyard enlivened with fountains, flowers, and a band that played on summer evenings. One of its earliest managers was an American, and the Langham was indeed a place which, with its resemblance to American hotels, made visitors from the States feel particularly at home. They came to it in great numbers, especially in the years following the Civil War. Owing to bomb damage, the building has not been used as an hotel since the Second World War, but rather as offices for the British Broadcasting Corporation, which, sadly, proposes to demolish it.

*Reception room in the Hôtel Intercontinental, Paris.*

By legislation passed in 1856 and 1862, the British Parliament facilitated the promotion of limited liability companies and thus became partly responsible for launching not only the Langham but also the 1860s boom in hotels and British business as a whole. The most grandiose of the numerous seaside hotels produced at this ebullient time was the Grand Hotel (1863-1867) at Scarborough, designed by Cuthbert Brodrick (1822-1905), whose Leeds Town Hall, a decade earlier, had been the country's most forceful expression of High Victorian civic pride. Boldly constructed on a sloping site, the Scarborough Grand rose on its beach side to an unbelievable thirteen storeys, their towering height further crowned with tall angle domes.

The English palace hotels seen thus far were mostly designed in a showy French-cum-Italian style inspired by the confident buildings of Second Empire Paris, for example the New Louvre built for Napoleon III by Visconti and Lefuel in 1852-1857. Both the style and the scale of such English hotels had their British parallel only in the design of warehouses and offices of the same period. However, one of the largest hotels, the Midland Grand at St. Pancras Station, in London, designed by Sir Gilbert Scott (1811-1878) to accommodate 400 guests, came forth as a paradigm of the extravagant romanticism of England's Gothic Revival. Built in 1868-1874 for over £ 400,000, the Midland was ingenuously described by its architect as 'possibly *too good* for its purpose'. Sir Gilbert further claimed that it 'was in the same style which I had almost originated several years earlier, for the government offices, but divested of the Italian element'.

Stylistically, the vast hotels erected in American cities in the 1850s and 60s had made little progress. The St. Nicholas Hotel (1851-1854), La Farge House (1854-1856), and the Fifth Avenue Hotel (1856-1859), all in New York, and the Lindell Hotel (1863) in St. Louis, Missouri, reflected the rather grim warehouse Italianate of many English railway hotels. La Farge House, however, boasted a cast-iron façade and iron pillars on the inside, which made it up-to-date with contemporary office and warehouse design in both Britain and the United States. The building of La Farge House was rushed forward so that it could cater for visitors to the Crystal Palace, opened in 1853 as the home of New York's first World's Fair. Alas, the hotel burned to the ground on its opening night, 8 January 1854, only to be rebuilt within two years. In Paris the Grand Hôtel du Louvre in the Rue de Rivoli was similarly put up in time for the opening of the second International Exhibition in 1855. The Grand entered history as the first hotel of its kind in Paris. Until its arrival, the quality hotels in the French capital, such as the Meurice and the Bristol, catered only for the very rich, whom they housed in suites of apartments. With the encouragement of Napoleon III, Émile and Isaac Péreire founded the Compagnie Immobilière des Hôtels et des Immeubles de la Rue de Rivoli, the celebrated street that had been begun under Napoleon I from designs by Percier and Fontaine. The Grand Hôtel du Louvre was designed by Alfred Armand, Jacques Hittorff, Charles Rohault de Fleury, and Auguste Pellechet, in a subdued Second Empire style that blended with the First Empire classicism of the Rue de Rivoli. It contained around 700 bedrooms but was subsequently turned into shops and replaced by a new building in 1926-1927 from designs by Georges Pellechet. Equal in size to the old Grand, but slightly richer in style, was the Grand Hôtel near the Paris Opéra, designed in 1861 by Armand for the same clients and to fit into a vast triangular site. A square *cour d'honneur* leads into the immense D-shaped *salle des fêtes* or dining room, sumptuously painted by Cuvelier, Millet, and Perraud, and carved by Hardoin, Benier, and Darvaut. Its luxuries included baths, electric bells, acoustic tiles, and service lifts, but not yet passenger lifts or elevators. In 1904 the Grand received an impressive new carriage entrance in the Rue Scribe, constructed from designs by L.-C. and A. Lacau, along with the domed Salon de Thé added by Nénot.

For the Paris Exhibition of 1878 the Hôtel Continental (today Inter-Continental) was built in the Rue de Rivoli on the corner of the Rue de Castiglione, once occupied by the Ministère des Finances until put to the Communard torch in 1871. Designed by Henri Blondel (1832-1897), the Continental offered magnificent Second Empire interiors, including a Grand Salon inspired by Garnier's foyer at the Paris Opéra. All elements of the ensemble are now registered as Monuments Historiques. Finally, we should note the Hôtel du Palais d'Orsay, built in 1898-1900 as part of the new Gare du Quai d'Orsay, which, like the hotel, was put up to coincide with the Paris Exhibition of 1900. The Palais d'Orsay also took over a site emptied by the Communards, this time to get rid of the Cour des Comptes. Designed by the architect Victor Laloux (1850-1937), the new hostelry was one of Paris's most baroque extravaganzas.

Elsewhere in Europe we should note Baron Carl Schwartz 1863-1866 Österreichischer Hof in Salzburg and the exactly contemporary, but far larger, Amstel Hotel in Amsterdam, designed by Cornelis Outshoorn in a French Second Empire mode. Visited by the Dutch royal family in the year of its opening, 1867, the Amstel has been favoured by royalty ever since. By then the Swiss had already been developing their resorts. Zurich's Baur en Ville dates from as early as 1836 (but enlarged in 1907), and the same city's Baur au Lac from eight years later (then enlarged in 1852, 1877, and 1896). Vevey got the Grand Hôtel des Trois Couronnes in 1843, Lucerne the Schweizerhof in 1845-1846 (rebuilt in 1885), Lausanne-Ouchy the Beau Rivage Palace in 1858-1861 (enlarged in 1908), Lucerne the Grand Hôtel du Lac in 1868 (rebuilt in 1897), as well as the Grand Hôtel National in 1871 (enlarged in 1900). The Riviera came into its own in the 1860s as a place of resort during the winter, when Homburg and the casinos in Germany were shut. The Casino at Monte Carlo opened in 1863 and the Hôtel de Paris, next door, in the following year. Designed by Dutrou, who took his inspiration from the architecture of the Grand near the Paris Opéra, the Hôtel de Paris has been rebuilt no less than seven times.

During the 1870s, hotels in America, especially in New York, Chicago, St. Louis, and San Francisco, simply grew larger and larger, while in Europe the Franco-American type of hotel became more and more widely established. It arrived in Vienna, for example, as part of the deliberate attempt to make the imperial capital resemble Napoleon III's Paris. Architecturally, the generative feature of the new Vienna was the building of the Ringstrasse, a broad, circular boulevard that, beginning in 1858, took form on the site of the old city fortifications. Grandiose new hotels appeared in the early 1870s, among them the Britannia, on the Schillerplatz, and the Donau, both designed by H. Claus and J. Grosz ; the Metropole by K. Schumann and L. Tischler ; the Sacher, behind the Opera House, by W. Fraenkl ; and the Imperial, built in the Kärtner Ring in 1863-1865 by A. Zenetti and H. Adam as the town palace of Duke Philipp of Württemberg, and remodelled as an hotel in 1873 in time for the International Exhibition scheduled for that year. The Imperial, which still flourishes, was patronized from the first by the high aristocracy and royalty, including Emperor Franz Joseph himself, no doubt in considerable part because of the fact that it had not originated as an hotel but as a princely residence of fabulous magnificence.

Berlin got its first grand hotel when the Kaiserhof, built from designs by Hennicke and von der Hude, opened its doors in 1875. With only 232 rooms, the Kaiserhof was still small by American standards. A livelier project was the Frankfurter Hof (1872-1876) in Frankfurt, which Mylius and Bluntschli designed to be approached through an arcaded garden court.

The hotels we have seen so far, luxurious though they were for their day, could scarcely be considered architecturally festive in the way that palace hotels would become during their peak period from the 1880s to the 1920s. At the climax of this development, around 1900, the chief resorts with gigantic palace hotels, generally of indifferent architectural quality, were to be found in Switzerland, at St. Moritz, Gstaad, and Lucerne ; in the South of France, at Nice, Monte Carlo, Cannes, Biarritz, and Menton ; in Normandy, at Deauville, Le Touquet, and Cabourg ; in the French spa towns of Aix-les-Bains, Evian-les-Bains, Contrexéville, Vichy, and Vittel ; and in the German ones of Karlsbad, Baden-Baden, and many others. The fabled Brenner's Park Hotel at Baden-Baden counted among the many places where Edwardians recuperated from their rich and copious dining.

The most interesting example of hotel architecture in America in the 1880s was in a class all its own : the Auditorium Hotel in Adler and Sullivan's celebrated Auditorium Building, erected in 1887-1889 in Chicago. By the time of the disastrous fire of 1871, Chicago was already the metropolis of the Middle West, despite its lack of distinguished architecture. The situation, however, changed in the 1880s with the development of iron-frame construction, first attempted in Jenney's Home Life Insurance Building of 1883. In New York, office buildings run up during the previous decade had reached a height of twelve storeys measuring 250 feet, but the initiative now passed to Chicago, where the carrying of external walls on iron and eventually steel frames brought about the birth of the skyscraper. With its austere, rock-faced Romanesque style, the Marshall Field Wholesale Store built in 1885-1887 from a design by Henry Hobson Richardson established a method of articulation for multi-storey buildings that would soon be reinterpreted by Adler and Sullivan in their 1886 design for the Auditorium Building. This structure contained an auditorium with seats for over 4,000, an hotel for only 400 guests, and an opera house. Though he did not design any more hotels, Sullivan produced two fully developed skyscrapers, the Wainright Building (1890-1891) in St. Louis, Missouri, and the Guaranty Building (1894-1895) in Buffalo, N.Y., which were among the world's earliest high-rise steel-frame buildings. The type would revolutionize the construction and scale of grand hotels, beginning with such New York projects as the New Netherland (1893), the Savoy (1895), and the Manhattan (1896).

France during the 1880s saw the construction of the Hôtel Terminus adjoining the Gare St. Lazare in Paris. Designed by Juste Lisch (1828-1910), the station and hotel went into operation in May 1889, simultaneously with the opening of the Paris International Exhibition of that year. Though unremarkable on the outside, the hotel boasts a spectacular central hall surrounded by a two-storey arcade supported on coupled cast-iron columns. Lisch's Hôtel Terminus directly inspired the Pera Palace Hotel in Constantinople. England's turning point in that decade came with the river block of the Savoy Hotel, built in 1884-1889 for the impresario Richard D'Oyly

Carte. It was designed by T.E. Collcutt, with the Arts and Crafts architect A.H. Mackmurdo serving as consultant on interior decoration and furniture. Deliberately aimed at the American market, the Savoy was thus up-to-date in the American fashion, with fireproof construction incorporating steel joists encased in concrete, electric light throughout, six lifts, but still only 70 bathrooms for over 400 rooms. Moreover, it looked festive, being faced in white matt-glazed terracotta and completely wrapped about on all floors with balconies, as though the Thames on to which it looked were the warm, dancing waters of the Mediterranean. Another important feature of the Savoy was that it introduced into the history of grand hotels the name of César Ritz (1850-1918), who began managing the great hostelry in 1889, and was joined in 1890 by his brilliant chef, Auguste Escoffier. In the 1870s Ritz had been manager of the Grand Hôtel National at Lucerne, before moving on in the next decade to the Grand Hôtel at Monaco and the Hôtel de Provence at Cannes. Here the Prince of Wales, the future Edward VII, and the gilded aristocracy of England and the Continent, who would not have been seen dead in hotels in England, enjoyed themselves tremendously, undetected by censorious eyes and cosseted in comfort unobtainable in English hotels at that time.

In 1893 the Savoy Hotel Company bought Claridge's in Brook Street, an architecturally modest but socially select hotel fitted into a row of houses in the middle of Mayfair. After more than a half-century of discreetly catering for the upper classes, Claridge's was now completely rebuilt from designs by an obscure architect called C.W. Stephens. The many-dormered red-brick pile this produced was consistent with the style in which noblemen, bored by the Georgian restraint of Mayfair, were rebuilding their private houses in the surrounding streets. The new hotel's lavishly decorated main reception areas, however, came from the more fashionable firm of Sir Ernest George & Yates, and they partly survive beneath an elegantly classical Art Deco veneer, applied in the course of a remodelling carried out in 1930-1931 by Oswald Milne.

Elsewhere in Mayfair rose the Coburg Hotel (later known as the Connaught), built in 1894-1896 in a similar, rather amorphous style from designs by Isaacs and Florence. The Hotel Cecil, constructed on the Thames Embankment next to the Savoy in 1890-1896 by Archer and Green, claimed to be the largest hotel in Europe, with its 800 bedrooms and its 100-foot-long ballroom capable of accommodating 600 dancers. Beneath the big square-based French domes, however, the Cecil's towering façades brought little more architectural sophistication or cheer to London than did the monster railway hotels of the 1860s. Nor, architecturally, was the Carlton Hotel of 1897-1899 much of an improvement, though it did provide a bathroom to every bedroom for the first time in London. The Carlton had been built in the Haymarket by the architect C.J. Phipps as part of a large group that included Her Majesty's Theatre. Prior to completion, however, the shell was acquired by the Carlton Hotel Company, which included César Ritz and Lord de Grey, a close friend of the Prince of Wales. They employed Isaacs and Florence to finish the hotel ; more importantly, they recruited the brilliant French architect Charles Mewès (1858-1914) to design the principal interiors : the Palm Court and the Dining and Grill Rooms. The organization of an hotel's main circulation spaces round a palm court or winter garden, so much a feature of Edwardian hotel life, seems to have originated with César Ritz.

The success of London's Savoy had already led to the establishment by the Savoy Hotel Company of the Grand Hotel in the Via Vittorio Emanuele in Rome. Designed as a splendidly forbidding sixteenth-century Roman palazzo by the architect Giulio Podesti, under the direction of Ritz and Escoffier, the Rome Grand opened with great panache at a reception on 11 January 1894. Ritz soon began planning his own ideal hotel in Paris, to be named after himself. Designed by Charles Mewès, the Paris Ritz, inaugurated in June 1898, was so luxurious and exclusive that it looked less like an hotel than the town residence of an eighteenth-century nobleman. Ritz and Mewès achieved this effect by building behind Jules Hardouin-Mansart's elegant 1698 façades in the Place Vendôme. It is thus untypical of grand hotels, which have nearly always been specially built, with the notable exception of the Danieli in Venice, made out of a fourteenth-century palazzo in 1822, and the sixteenth-century Villa d'Este at Cernobbio on Lake Como, which became an hotel in 1873.

Paris had lagged behind London in the planning and construction of luxury hotels, but the situation changed dramatically around 1900, particularly with a group of hotels built between the Opéra and the Étoile. In 1898 the leading hotel architect Georges Chédanne (1861-1940) built the Palace Hotel in the Champs-Élysées, adopting the grand Rococo style of his French Embassy in Vienna. Erected for the Compagnie des Wagons-Lits, it today houses the Crédit Commercial de France. In 1903 Chédanne built the Hôtel Mercédès on the corner of the Avenue Kléber and the Rue de Presbourg, for once eschewing the Louis XVI style in favour of a plastically fluid composition verging on Art Nouveau. The style shortly blossomed in the colourful Hôtel Luté-

tia, built in 1910 in the Boulevard Raspail by the Société du Bon-Marché with L. Boileau and M. Tauzin as architects and Binet as sculptor. In plan, the Hôtel Mercédès, with its long, narrow layout and central winter garden, is not unlike the London Ritz. Today it shelters the Société Kléber-Colombes.

Also in the Avenue Kléber near the Etoile rose the 400-bedroom Hôtel Majestic designed in 1908 in a monumental Louis XVI manner by M.-A. Sibien, with Dumas and Alavoine responsible for the interior decoration. The Majestic occupied the site of the Hôtel Basilewsky, a sumptuous private house erected for a Russian collector in 1864 and subsequently occupied by the Queen of Spain. Tauber, the proprietor of the Hôtel Majestic, also founded the Hôtel Régina, where in 1903 he employed the same architect, Sibien, to construct elegant interiors behind the existing façade in the Rue St. Honoré and the Place des Pyramides near the Louvre. In the same fashionable neighbourhood are to be found two of the most luxurious hotels in Europe : the Hôtel Meurice in the Rue de Rivoli and the Hôtel de Crillon in the Place de la Concorde. The Meurice had come into being as early as 1817, but in 1905 it fell into the hands of new owners, who employed Paul-Henri Nénot (1853-1934), the distinguished architect of the new Sorbonne (1885-1901), to enlarge and transform it. The new wing that Nénot added facing on to the Rue du Mont-Thabor is in his own somewhat heavy classical manner. More sophisticated was the remodelling in 1912 of the Hôtel de Crillon, built by Gabriel in 1755-1776. After acquiring the property in 1907, the Société des Grands Magasins et des Hôtels du Louvre enlarged the site and employed the architect Walter Destailleur to remodel the hotel. The exquisite interiors installed by Destailleur include a columnar staircase in a convincing Louis XVI style, but some of Gabriel's original interiors went to the Hôtel de la Tour d'Auvergne, which was then being built from designs by René Sergent and today houses the Chilean Embassy.

Neither the Paris Ritz nor the London Carlton occupied buildings that Ritz had commissioned. The opportunity for him to express his ideals simultaneously in architecture, interior design, and hotel management came in 1902 with the purchase by his financial backers of the Walsingham House Hotel and adjacent Bath Hotel in Piccadilly. Though a recent building of great height on concrete foundations, Walsingham House was demolished as insufficiently elegant to meet Ritz's requirements. On its site next to Green Park there arose in 1904-1905, from the designs of Mewès and his young English partner, Arthur Davis (1878-1951), one of the most perfect luxury hotels in the world.

The London Ritz rests upon a plan beautifully and lucidly organized round one of César Ritz's palm courts, opening from a broad lateral corridor, while the decoration and furnishing throughout adheres to the Louis XVI style. From the start, this gave the building a visual coherence and refinement lacking in most grand hotels, which were decorated either in a more showy style altogether, or in a range of contrasting 'period' styles, like those devised for Norman Shaw's

*Reception room in the* Grand Hôtel, *Paris.*

nearby Piccadilly Hotel of 1905. Even the Paris Ritz had been decorated in a number of styles, from Louis XIV to the First Empire. Albeit well integrated in their ensemble, the façades of the London Ritz evoke a variety of Parisian structures, including the arcaded Rue de Rivoli, while the hotel's construction marked a turning point in the history of English architecture as the first instance of the type of steel frame that had been pioneered by the Chicagoans in the 1880s. The technical advantages of the system made it possible for a building to rise higher and on lighter foundations and be completed in a far shorter time, since the load of the upper portions was carried by the interlocking beams of a steel cage, rather than by the strength of the wall mass at the bottom. As an indication of the novelty of this structural system, the Swedish-born Sven Bylander, who had already had building experience in the United States, was appointed consulting engineer for the steel work, which was itself manufactured in Germany.

In the meantime, the Savoy Hotel was extended with a large new block along the Strand. Executed in 1903-1904 from designs by T.E. Collcutt and S. Hamp, the new Savoy incorporated a great deal of steel, constructed under the supervision of an American firm of contractors. Next came the Waldorf Hotel (1905-1907) in Aldwych by A.M. and A.G.R. Mackenzie, with a steel frame designed by Sven Bylander. This building still retains its original Palm Court, and, as though to underline the Edwardian love of carefree entertainment, it was and remains flanked by two contemporary theatres, the Waldorf (now the Strand) and the Aldwych.

The combination of steel frame and Louis XVI ornament used at the Ritz proved no less suitable for office buildings when Mewès and Davis erected the *Morning Post* offices in 1905-1907 on a site near the Waldorf Hotel. In 1908-1911 they extended the same principles to club design with the Royal Automobile Club, Pall Mall. Mewès, with his partner Bischoff, turned to the great ocean-going liners of the Cunard and Hamburg-Amerika lines, transforming them into floating hotels of unbelievable luxury, beginning with the interiors designed in 1903 for the *Amerika*, the finest liner then afloat. In 1912 Mewès and Bischoff designed the even more splendid *Imperator* for the Kaiser, while in the following year Davis designed the *Aquitania*. In 1908-1910 Mewès, in collaboration with Luis Landecho, designed another Ritz Hotel, this time in Madrid, producing yet one more superb Edwardian luxury hotel. It was promoted by the Ritz Development Company, founded in 1908 with the support of the twenty-two-year-old King of Spain, Alfonso XIII, who wanted an hotel in his capital city equal to those he had seen and admired on his Grand Tour.

Perhaps London's most monumental example of classical architecture hung on a Chicago-type steel cage is Selfridge's store in Oxford Street, built in 1907-1928 from designs by two American architects, Daniel Burnham of Chicago and Francis Sales, with assistance from the English architect Frank Atkinson and the Scottish architect J.J. Burnet. It was Atkinson who also planned one of the finest Edwardian luxury hotels in England, the 1908-1914 Adelphi at Liverpool, its restrained Neoclassical style already pointing forward to the greater austerity of architecture in the 1920s and 1930s. The moving genius behind this vast steel-framed hotel was Sir William Towle, manager of the Midland Railway Company since 1884, who built two hotels for the company, the Midland at Manchester in 1897-1903, designed by Charles Trubshaw, and the Adelphi at Liverpool. In 1904 the Palm Court of the Manchester hotel provided the setting for the first encounter of Charles Rolls and Henry Royce.

Turn-of-the-century designers of grand hotels found another structural innovation in reinforced-concrete frame construction. One of the pioneers of the method was François Hennebique (1842-1921), whose 1900 Imperial Palace Hotel at Nice was the first hotel to be constructed of reinforced concrete. With its fifteen storeys, the Imperial Palace also became the largest such building in the world. It was followed in 1905 by the gigantic Marlborough-Blenheim Hotel in Atlantic City, New Jersey, designed in reinforced concrete by the Philadelphia architects Price and McLanahan. Though the structural frame would have allowed a façade of whatever durable material the architect might have chosen, the Marlborough-Blenheim was actually given a cladding of ornamented concrete. One of the first buildings in unreinforced concrete was the 1887 Ponce de Leon Hotel at St. Augustine, Florida, designed in the Spanish Colonial style to evoke the town's historical importance as the earliest Spanish mission in Florida. Albeit arrière-garde in its embellishments, the Ponce de Leon looked to the future not only in its structural system, but also by becoming one of the first American hotels to adopt electric light on a large scale. In terms of major work, it also marked the debut of Carrère and Hastings, both of whom had been trained at the École des Beaux-Arts in Paris. The partners went on to produce some of the finest classical buildings in America, including the New York Public Library (1897-1911).

Another record shattered when the sixteen-storey steel-and-concrete Waldorf-Astoria Hotel (1890-1897) offered its clients 1,000 rooms, the first New York hotel to attain that capacity. Designed by H.J. Hardenbergh, the Waldorf contained numerous suites for resident industrialists, Pittsburgh steel millionaires, and Wall Street adventurers, who found it easier to entertain there than in private houses. It was demolished in 1929, to make way for the Empire State Building. Another towering New York hotel with many permanent residents, perhaps of greater social prestige, was the Plaza, opened in 1907 after having been built from designs by that hotel specialist H.J. Hardenbergh. Undoubtedly one of the most glamorous hotels in the world, the Plaza is lavishly enriched with fittings and decoration in different historical styles. Shipped from Europe, the décor gives an impression of old-world luxury very different from the fastidious restraint of Mewès and Davis at the London Ritz.

Hotel designers did not often feel free before the First World War to depart from the gilded palatial style, probably derived from the work of Charles Garnier, a style that had become the norm for Grand Hotels throughout Europe around 1900. The billowing Baroque interiors of Stoecklin's Hotel Gallia (1899 ; now demolished) at Cannes may stand as the perfect expression of the type. Exceptions coalesce into two main stylistic categories : Art Nouveau, already hinted at in the Hôtel Gallia, and national, as in America's Georgian Colonial designs. The emphasis on nature and on craftsmanship originated with writers like Ruskin who, by reacting against nineteenth-century industrialization, helped bring about the stunning architectural and decorative style known as Art Nouveau. In Italy, where it especially flourished under the name *Stile Floreale*, the style received an elaborate treatment in the Hotel Tre Croce at Campo dei Fiori near Varese, built in 1907-1912 from designs by Giuseppe Sommaruga (1867-1917). With its V-shaped plan and its far-projecting, Piranesi-like arcuated porch, this was the last and most grandiose work of the leading Art Nouveau architect of Italy.

Other centres of Art Nouveau include Paris, where we might note some interiors in Sibien's Hôtel Régina (1903), and Moscow, whose Hotel Metropol (1899-1903) emerged as a fancifully Art Nouveau monument by William Walcot (1874-1943), who had been born in Odessa of a Russian mother and an English father. A brilliant architectural draughtsman, Walcot settled in London in c. 1907 and there became the leading perspective artist of his day. In Berlin the architects of the Adlon Hotel (1905-1907), C. Gause and R. Leibnitz, created a strange but rich atmosphere in which an Art Nouveau flavour combined with references derived from Karl Friedrich Schinkel (1781-1841), the greatest architect of Neoclassical Berlin.

As for national styles, the Iberian peninsula offers examples of revivalist designs in Barcelona's Hotel Internacional (1888 ; now demolished), with its Catalan Gothic manner designed by Lluis Domenech I. Montaner (1850-1923), and in the astonishing Hotel Bussaco near Coimbra, Portugal, a neo-Manueline Gothic extravaganza begun in 1887 from designs by Luigi Manini as a villa for the Portuguese royal family.

In the United States the return to a Georgian Colonial style occurred in a representative manner at the Greenbrier Hotel in White Sulphur Springs, Virginia, which opened to guests in September 1913. A vast pile designed by the New York architect Frederick Julius Sterner, it struck a popular note that would be increasingly echoed in a wide range of building types. In 1919 the Greenbrier was visited by the Prince of Wales, later Edward VIII, whose future wife, Wallis Warfield, had already spent the first of her three honeymoons in it. As Duke and Duchess of Windsor, the couple were to pass much of their life together in the grand hotels of Europe and America, thereby attempting to compensate for the splendour from which they had been cut off by Edward's abdication.

Certainly the 1920s saw little diminution in the quality of grand hotel life. In America hotels were now built for the first time in the skyscraper form developed for office buildings, for example, the Stevens (1927 ; now Conrad Hilton) in Chicago by J.A. Holabird, and the far more striking new Waldorf-Astoria (1930-1931) in New York by Schulze and Weaver. With its 46 storeys rising above Park Avenue, its 2,253 bedrooms all wired for radio and television, its four ballrooms and extensive roof gardens, the Waldorf-Astoria, like so many hotels before it, was intended to be the last word in luxury. However, it would soon be rivalled by the more residential character of the Hotel Pierre (1929-1930), overlooking Central Park from Fifth Avenue. A 42-storey skyscraper designed by Schulze and Weaver, the Pierre lacked the showy public rooms of the Plaza and the Waldorf-Astoria but offered half its accommodations to permanent residents. Something of the discreet elegance of the Pierre also touched the Ritz-Carlton, opened in 1927 in the most attractive part of Boston.

Paris saw the opening in 1928 of the George V, designed by Lefranc and Wibo in the modern streamlined style, in contrast to the more exuberantly classical architecture of its principal rival, the Plaza-Athénée, a 1913 structure in the Avenue Montaigne. The cellars of the George V occupy part of the quarry that had supplied the stone for the Arc de Triomphe. In postwar London the collapse of aristocratic life on the old Victorian scale was expressed in the demolition of the great town mansions in Mayfair. Like the Hotel Pierre, which stands on the site of one of the great New York mansions, the Grosvenor Hotel (1926-1928) sadly took the place of Grosvenor House, the early-nineteenth-century town residence of the Dukes of Westminster. Though Wimperis, Simpson and Guthrie prepared the plans for this giant new hotel in Park Lane, it was the more dazzling Sir Edwin Lutyens who designed the façades, making his most spectacular contribution in the arched pavilions on the skyline. Unfortunately, they are so far above the street level as to be lost on most viewers. Moreover, the hotel represents a decline from the classical façades in Portland stone that Lutyens designed in the 1920s for steel-frame office buildings in the City of London, such as the Midland Bank in Poultry and Britannic (now Lutyens) House in Finsbury Circus.

Farther along Park Lane, the Dorchester Hotel (1929-1930) rose on the site of one of the finest nineteenth-century classical buildings in England, Dorchester House, built by Vulliamy in 1850-1863 for the millionaire collector Rober Stayner Holford. With the long shallow curve of its south front, the Dorchester is a more elegant essay in restrained modernism than the George V in Paris. On a reinforced-concrete frame designed by the engineer Sir Owen Williams, the talented architect William Curtis Green (1875-1960) hung a skin of pre-cast terrazzo panels punctuated by continuous cantilevered balconies, which, thanks to the concrete frame, did not require supporting brackets. Though trained in the Arts and Crafts tradition, Curtis Green designed in a sophisticated classical style. The combination of modern structural techniques with elements from the two stylistic traditions, as well as with a certain amount of Art Deco in the predominantly classical interiors, reaped praise even from the architect M.H. Baillie Scott (1865-1945), high priest of the Arts and Crafts movement. In 1931 Baillie Scott described the Dorchester as 'the only modernist building I have seen which, while owing little or nothing to tradition in its outward aspect, yet contrives to appear gracious and friendly. It has none of the brutal logical "take-it-or-leave-it" aspect with which we are familiar in modernist buildings'. In structure, decoration, and function — for it has had permanent residents from the start — the Dorchester Hotel can be regarded as a final development of many of the themes noted in the last few pages. Inaugurated in 1930, the terminal date for this book, it forms a fitting conclusion to the opening chapter.

*Drawing of the façade of
the* Hotel Métropole, *Moscow.*
*Following pages:*
*left-*Palace Hôtel, *St. Moritz.*
*right-*Palace Hotel, *Bussaco.*

# ACT I
# BUILDING A DREAM

3

2    4

5

6

32

1 and 2 - *Sitting Room and staircase of the* Danieli, *Venice // This hotel, like the Paris* Ritz, *the* Villa d'Este *and a few others, is something of an exception since, rather than being built as an hotel, it was originally a C.14th palazzo of the Dandolo family and was converted for hotel use in 1822. Famous for harboring George Sand and Alfred de Musset during their love affair, the* Danieli *was much favored by Balzac, Wagner, Proust and Gabriele D'Annunzio.*

3 and 4 - *Ballroom and Reading Room of the* Grand Hôtel, *Paris // The building of the* Grand Hôtel *was part of Haussmann's vast improvement programme for the city of Paris. On the initiative of Napoleon III and taking the large London hotels as a model, the* Grand Hôtel du Louvre, *rue de Rivoli, was built first, followed seven years later by the* Grand Hôtel, *Place de l'Opéra. At the time the latter was considered to be the largest hotel in Europe. The inauguration, on the 14th of July, 1862, occasioned the Empress Eugénie's charming remark: "It's just like home".*

5, 6 and 7 - *Interiors and façade, link pavilion of the* Beau Rivage *hotel at Ouchy.* 10 - *General view // Opened in 1861, the* Beau Rivage *with its 150 bedrooms, vast reception rooms and Bath House, achieved an international reputation. The accommodation rapidly proved insufficient and, in 1905, work on a new hotel started on an adjoining site and was completed in 1907. At the same time a dog cemetery was laid out in the grounds lest the guests should be bereaved of their canine friends. The 1861 and 1907 buildings are joined by the link pavilion.*

8 - *The* Grand Hotel, *Scarborough, North Yorkshire // The* Grand Hotel *opened in 1867 as a result of the development of the North Sea resorts. Built of yellow and red brick, the hotel only catered for the July-August season.*

9 - *A view of the* Villa d'Este *on the shores of Lake Como, prior to its 1873 conversion into a hotel // The villa was originally built in 1561 for Cardinal Tolomeo Gallio.*

11 and 12 - *The arrival of the stage coach at the* Hôtel Royal, *San Remo, built in 1872, with a late C.19th advertisement.*

11

HOTEL ROYAL SAN REMO

13 - *The main courtyard of the* Hôtel Continental *when accessible to carriage traffic.* 15 - *The Moorish Saloon. According to an old advertisement, it reproduced "with exactitude the marvels of the Alhambra".*

16 - *A ball in the grand reception room.// Built for the Paris World Fair of 1878, the* Hôtel Continental *has since become the Intercontinental. Blondel, the hotel's architect, was later to design the Bourse de Commerce (Commodities Exchange) and the Belle Jardinière department store. The influence of Charles Garnier is apparent in the design of the drawing room, directly inspired by the foyer of the Paris Opéra (Garnier was Blondel's father-in-law). The artists commissioned for the interior decoration also created the decor of the famous "Train Bleu", the restaurant of the Gare de Lyon. Many important literary, political and artistic events took place here. On the 25th of February, 1883, Victor Hugo, then well over eighty, presided at the last banquet given in his honor.*

14 - *The* Hôtel d'Angleterre *Crystal Court, Copenhagen, where the orchestra continuously played chamber music.// This hotel has had a long and erratic history. In the C.18th a French barber, Jean Maréchal, married the daughter of King Frederic V's Chef. Some years later, in 1755, he opened his own restaurant in the King's New Square and business flourished thanks to his wife's connections. In 1787 the restaurant was sold to a Berliner, Gottfried Rau, becoming the Hotel Rau, but was destroyed in the disastrous fire which ravaged Copenhagen in 1795. Rau then acquired one of the few surviving buildings, the splendid town house of the Grams family and opened it as the* Hôtel d'Angleterre, *so named in honor of the English Club of which he was a member. Altered in the C.19th, the hotel was inaugurated in its final form on the 5th of May, 1875. Queen Juliana of the Netherlands, who had the famous first-floor suite was unable to refrain from exclaiming : "All this just for me!"*

13

14

15

16

17 and 18 - *The*
Schwarzer Bock Hotel,
*Wiesbaden: the corridor ser-*
*ving the bath cubicles and*
*the dining room of the*
*French Restaurant.// Origi-*
*nally a modest country inn*
*dating back to 1486, the*
Schwarzer Bock *was ac-*
*quired in 1834 by its present*
*owners, the Schäfer family.*
*The Schäfers benefited from*
*the rapid expansion of*
*Wiesbaden, capital from*
*1806 of the Duchy of Nas-*
*sau, then, following its an-*
*nexation by Prussia, a holi-*
*day resort of the Prussian*
*princes. Wiesbaden became a*
*spa of international renown.*
*The hotel was reorganized*
*in 1870. In 1905 and 1924,*
*it was again subject to*
*considerable alterations.*
*This series of improvements*
*reveals the successive adap-*
*tation of this spa hotel to*
*meet the needs of the ever*
*increasing clientele taking*
*the waters.* The Schwarzer
Bock, *like other such spa*
*establishments, had to ex-*
*pand and provide the equip-*
*ment required by modern hy-*
*drotherapy and achieve a*
*synthesis of treatment and*
*pleasure, that eternal duality*
*of the spa town.*
19 - *The* Hôtel Imperial,
*Vienna// In 1867, Philip*
*Duke of Württemberg had a*
*palace built in Vienna*
*which he never occupied. For*
*the Vienna Exhibition of*
*1873 the Württemberg pa-*
*lace was converted to a hotel*
*and named* The Imperial
*by the Emperor Franz-*
*Joseph himself. The Exhibi-*
*tion and the reputation of*
*the hotel attracted so many*
*visitors that from the year of*
*its inauguration onward it*
*was never to lack for book-*
*ings. The influx of guests of*
*the highest rank was not*
*without its diplomatic prob-*
*lems; thus, while Bismarck*
*and Mac-Mahon agreed ex-*
*ceptionally to "lodge at the*
*same inn", they categori-*
*cally refused to share the*
*same floor. In 1875 Wagner*
*stayed at the* Imperial *for*
*two months while complet-*
*ing "Tannhaüser". After*
*the collapse of the Austro-*
*Hungarian Empire, the ho-*
*tel diversified its clientele*
*and opened its doors to the*
*new aristocracy of finance.*
*Hard times began in 1938.*
*The* Hôtel Imperial *was*
*requisitioned by the Third*
*Reich and Hitler stayed*
*there a number of times. In*
*ruins at the end of the war,*
*the hotel served as Russian*
*headquarters until 1955.*
*The hotel was then restored.*

19

20

21

22

# DINING ROOM
# GRAND HÔTEL DE LA PAIX
## GENEVA

On the memorable occasion, when the Court of Arbitrators held its sittings at Geneva in 1872, to decide upon the «Alabama» claims, the arduous labours of the Court were not unfrequently interrupted by dinners of ceremony or hospitality, offered by Switzerland to the guests. The farewell banquet given to the members of the Court by the Conseil d'Etat of the Canton of Geneva, was amongst the most brilliant and successful. It was held in the Hotel de la Paix of Geneva;

The large room as well as the spacious and beautiful outer hall being splendidly decorated for the occasion. M. Carteret, President of the Conseil d'Etat and Chairman of the evening, thanked the Arbitrators for having honoured Geneva by selecting it for the place of meeting, whilst Count Sclopis, as President of the Court reciprocated the compliment by thanking the people of Geneva for their kind welcome. The above scene represents the guests at the moment when the Count is delivering his speech.

Banquet given to the Alabama arbitrators by the Geneva Conseil d'Etat, Saturday 7 September 1872.
Count Sclopis reading his speech.

# GRAND HÔTEL DE CANNES
## ( ALPES MARITIMES. )

20 and 21 - On the 11th of February, 1882, an international billiards match was held in the reception rooms of the Grand Hôtel, Paris. As the games progressed the winners' scores appeared on the hotel's Place de l'Opéra façade.

22 - The kitchens of the Grand Hôtel du Louvre// Planning to organize the World Fair of 1855, Napoleon III persuaded the Pereire brothers to finance the first Parisian grand hotel, offering a 30 year tax exemption on the hotel in exchange. On this basis, work on the Grand Hôtel du Louvre duly started. Because of the very tight schedule, building went on day and nights thanks to powerful electric lamps, their novelty attracting bystanders. The hotel welcomed its first guests on the 16th of October, 1855, and had 800 bedrooms, a first class restaurant, reception rooms, reading rooms and "by a praiseworthy innovation, numerous bathrooms". The Grands Magasins du Louvre (a department store) was installed at the same time in the rue Marengo. This store gradually absorbed the whole first floor of the hotel, the mezzanine and then the second floor. The Grand Hôtel du Louvre finally moved to its present site on the other side of the Place du Palais-Royal, while the store took over the whole building.

23 - In the C 19th during the American Civil War, the English built Confederate privateer the "Alabama" wreaked heavy losses on the Union's merchant fleet. A demand for compensation was made by the United States government and Switzerland acted as mediator. On the 7th of September, 1872, the Council of State of the Republic and Canton of Geneva invited the members of the adjudicating court to a dinner at the Grand Hôtel de la Paix. This historic menu can still be served today in the hotel's restaurant.

24 - The Grand Hôtel, Cannes, opened in 1864 // "A hotel nearly as large as the Louvre one and always full, has been built on the seashore". (Prosper Mérimée)

25 - *General view of the* Midland Hotel *and St. Pancras Station, London.* 26 - *The staircase and (inset the) hotel entrance // In the first half of the C.19th, grand hotels and railway stations are two architectural innovations frequently found associated with each other. In Britain, where the railways were a determining factor in hotel development, the phenomenon is more noticeable than elsewhere. The* Midland *was thus built in front of the St. Pancras train shed, incorporating station offices on its first floor. This enormous Gothic Revival building, costing the seemingly exorbitant sum of £ 438,000, was still incomplete when it opened to the public in 1873. The hotel continued in use until 1935 and now it houses British Rail offices.*

26

45

27

28

46

31

32

27 - *The* Hôtel des Anglais, *Nice, built in 1875.*
28 - *The* Hôtel Continental *and the* Hôtel de l'Océan *on the sea wall at Ostend //* "*The sea wall dominates a large beach covered with a carpet of fine soft sand, strewn at low tide with all kinds of shells, enlivened by the horse-drawn bathing machines coming and going amidst the clutter of innumerable beach tents and awnings and the milling crowd of strollers. To sweep the beach at a single glance one has to place oneself beyond the Kursaal at the bend in the western sea wall. One can bathe at any time but preferably in the early morning or the latter part of the afternoon, with the incoming tide: ladies and gentlemen bathe together.*" *(From the "Illustrated Blue Guide").*
29 - *The* Amstel Hotel, *Amsterdam.*
30 - *Edward VII at the window of the* Hôtel Bristol, *Place Vendôme, Paris // Work on the building started in 1718 for John Law the banker, but, forced to flee after his bankruptcy, Law did not see its completion. It then became in 1720 the residence of the Regent's official mistress, Madame de Parabère, and was converted to hotel use in 1878.*
31 - *The* Grand Hôtel du Louvre et de la Paix, *Marseille : the interior courtyard.*
32 - *Carriages in front of the* Metropole Hotel, *London, in a photograph of 1905 // Situated in Northumberland Avenue, the* Metropole *opened in 1885. Frederick Gordon, the proprietor, already owned another establishment in the same street, the* Grand Hotel, *completed four years earlier.*

49

34

35

33 - *A corridor in the* Grand Hôtel, *Biarritz (1890) // The Empress Eugénie's liking for sea bathing started the development of seaside resorts on the Gascony Coast. To please her, Napoléon III built the famous Villa Eugénie at Biarritz in 1854, which became later the Hôtel du Palais. This was the beginning of Biarritz's fashionable renown, a resort where people met as much for social enjoyment as to benefit from the restorative virtues of the climate.*

34 and 35 - *Reception hall and a bedroom in the* Hôtel Métropole, Cannes. *Built in 1883, this 200-bedroom hotel was sold to the archdiocese in the 1930's and for many years accommodated a seminary before being demolished in 1975 // In 1834, when Lord Brougham happened to spend some time in the region, Cannes was little more then a fishing village. He was on his way to Italy but had been unable to cross the border as the King of Piedmont had declared a quarantine to control a cholera epidemic. Enjoying the sea, the sun and the mimosa, Lord Brougham decided to settle in Cannes and had the "Château Eléonore" built where he invited close friends to visit him. The lead given by Brougham and his circle opened up Cannes and over subsequent decades the town received such well-known British visitors as Turner, John Ruskin, Oscar Wilde, Rudyard Kipling and Bernard Shaw. It only needed Queen Victoria to crown the fame of the new resort and she duly came with her two sons. Henceforth the vogue for Cannes swelled at a prodigious rate. The opening of the P.L.M. railway line in 1864 was an important contributory factor in the town's expansion.*

36 and 37 - *The main staircase of the* Riviera Palace, Menton // Winter was the season when the delights of the Côte d'Azur were most appreciated, but even then tourists took all sorts of precautions to protect themselves from the sun: "We recommend strollers to wear light woollen materials, to have an overcoat and even a muffler and never to linger in the sun without a parasol". (From the "Guide Joanne" of 1910).*

37

38 and 39 - *The kitchens and wine cellar of the* Grand Hôtel, *Paris.*
40 - *The Ticket Office provided a world-wide information service: international exchange rates, liner and train arrival and departure times, weather forecasts, liner passenger lists, etc.*
41 and 42 - *The Plant Room with its electricity generators. These views show the control panels with their circuit dials and the boiler // The comparison frequently made between the transatlantic liners and the C.19th grand hotels is ideally suited to the* Grand Hôtel *in Paris. With its vast size, (10,000 sq. yards in plan) its legion staff — over 600 in 1895 — and its organization, the* Grand Hôtel *had all the self-sufficient traits of a ship at sea. Designed to accommodate all Europe, this establishment of 800 bedrooms and 65 reception rooms was, from its inception, equipped with the most up-to-date technology. Electric light, backed up by 4,000 gas jets, was provided throughout the hotel by the generators in the basement, which also supplied electricity for the telegraph and bells. The* Grand Hôtel *also had a hydraulic lift, elevators to convey the luggage to the bedrooms, and its own ice-making machine. The kitchens could cater for more than 2,000 diners, entailing a daily supply of some 500 chickens, hundreds of kilos of meat, more than 100 gallons of milk, tons of ice cream, etc.*
43, 44 and 45 - *"I dedicate these hotel bills to those who in the future may be interested and to those here and now who may be desirous of enlightenment on the practical side of things." (Exerpt from Felix Regamey's book "D'Aix en Aix" published in 1897.)*

38

39

40

41

42

54

No. 264    Dresden, den 20. 9.    1895

# Sendig's Hôtel Europäischer Hof.
## Rudolf Sendig.

Um Irrthümer zu vermeiden, werden die Rechnungen
täglich überreicht.
Pour éviter des erreurs on donne la note tous les jours.
To prevent mistakes bills are given daily.

Man bittet, die Rechnungen wöchentlich zu berichtigen.
On est prié de payer la note toutes les semaines.
Visitors are requested to settle their account weekly.

| | Transport: | Mark | Pf. | Mark | Pf. |
|---|---|---|---|---|---|
| Pension | | | | | |
| Logement | | 3 | 50 | | |
| Dejeuner | Eier | | | | |
| Diner | | 4 | — | | |
| | 1/2 Braunberger | 1 | 25 | | |
| Equipage | | | | | |
| Bäder | | | | | |
| Dienerschafts-Zehrung | | | | | |
| | 1 mann | | 50 | | |
| 21/9 | 1 gejeuner | 1 | 25 | | |

**Betrag empfangen**

Casse des Europäischen H.G.

---

# HÔTEL DE L'EUROPE
## HEIDELBERG

GEBR. KÜPFER

NOTE pour Mons Regamey
No 57

| 1894 | | Omnibus: | | | | | |
|---|---|---|---|---|---|---|---|
| Sept. | 14 | Appartement, Service et Eclairage compris | | | 5 | | |
| | 15 | Appartement | | | 3 | | |
| | | 1 Café pl. | | | 1 | 40 | |
| | | 1 Sauk Sing | | | | 50 | |
| | | 1 Lampe | | | | | |
| | 16 | 1 Café pl. | | | 1 | 25 | |
| | | Voiture | | | | | |

Au rapport
Hôtel de l'Europe
Gebr. Küpfer

---

# HÔTEL STADT ROM LEIPZIG
## C. OERTGE

In schönster Lage an der Promenade, gegenüber dem neuen THEATER und in unmittelbarer Nähe der Post.

Près des Stations des chemins de fer pour DRESDE, BERLIN, HAMBOURG, Cologne et Francfort s/M.

Adjoining the DRESDEN, BERLIN, HAMBURG, Cologne and Francfort 9/M Railway Station.

Zimmer No 10.    # RECHNUNG    den Sept. 1895
Fol. 493 5

| | | | | |
|---|---|---|---|---|
| 28 | Rechnung No 25 Gepäckauslagen 10 | | 33 | |
| | 2 Gl. Milch | | 50 | |
| 29 | 1 Café | Logis | 1 | |
| | | | 2 | |
| | | | 3 | 84 |

46 and 47 - *The* Palace Hôtel, *Bussaco. Detail of the Hall and the main staircase // Bussaco, until 1834, was a monastic estate. The site was a magnificent one and the good monks of the order of the Descalced Carmelites had kept themselves busy each year by further endowing the already splendid Bussaco forest with rare species of trees. At the end of the C.19th, Emidio Novarro, the Minister of Public Works, suggested to King Charles the idea of building a modern grand hotel there with a pavilion reserved for visiting royalty. The design was entrusted to the architect Luigi Manini. Built on the remains of the monastery, the hotel is a curious composition with tower and turret flanked by a gallery of twelve Manueline arches and with an ogival arcaded rotunda opening on to the gardens. Portuguese Art Nouveau designers were commissioned for the interior decoration. Opened in 1909, it immediately became the place were to go and to be seen.*

48 - *The* Grand Hôtel, *Curia.*

49 - *The* Hôtel Kurhaus *at Scheveningen // The Hôtel Kurhaus opened in 1885 only to be devastated by fire in 1886. Yet a year later the hotel was rebuilt with 150 bedrooms and a grand saloon. The concert hall installed in 1920 was to be the setting for a whole series of memorable recitals and performances such as those of Edith Piaf, Maurice Chevalier, Marlene Dietrich, Bela Bartok, Maria Callas and more recently the Rolling Stones. A 1971 proposal to convert the building into a speculative block of luxury flats failed, thanks to the number of petitions objecting to the scheme.*

50 - *The* Grand Hôtel *(1889-91) at Roquebrune-Cap-Martin.*

51 - *The* Grand Hôtel International, *Barcelona. // Designed in 1888 by the Catalan Renaxiença architect Domenéch y Montaner for the Barcelona World Fair this innovative temporary hotel was built in 63 days only, making considerable use of system building, and demolished when the Fair closed.*

48

49

50

51

52 - *The* Hotel Cecil, *London, with the* Savoy *in the background // Work on the hotel began in 1890. The scheme had been initiated by a certain Jabez Balfour who in this instance was unable to meet his financial obligations and in 1895 was finally sentenced to 14 years in prison. The works were nevertheless brought to a successful conclusion. Opened in 1896, the Cecil was considered to be the largest European hotel of its day and to have cost as much to build as the Paris Opéra – hardly surprising therefore that its funding proved a somewhat painful business! The hotel had 1,029 bedrooms and, in addition, 2 full basement floors – one decorated in the Hindoo style, comprising a Grillroom, table d'hôte dining room, American Bar, Smoking Room, Barber's Saloon and Telegraph Room; the other floor having the Ballroom, scene of the famous banquet held to celebrate the Entente Cordiale. Closed in 1930, the Hotel Cecil was finally taken down in only 16 weeks.*

53 - *The* Hyde Park Hotel, *London with the stamp issued by the hotel // The building was initially designed as a block of flats, another scheme of Jabez Balfour's. Built in 1888, it was converted to hotel use, after a fire, in 1900.*

GRAND-HÔTEL
PARIS

57

58

54 - *A bathroom in the* Savoy Hotel, *London //* The impresario Richard D'Oyly Carte had a theatre built in 1881 on the site of the old Savoy Palace, between the Strand and the Embankment. Highly impressed by American hotels on his business trips to the United States, he decided to provide London with a similar establishment. By 1884, work had started on the Embankment site and involved a noteworthy early structural use of concrete. The building took 5 years to complete and the inaugural publicity brochure proudly offered the Savoy's guests: "Electric light everywhere and at all times. No gas. Large and luxurious lifts working without interruption. Corridors heated day and night. 70 bathrooms." 70 bathrooms! The contractor, when informed of this feature, asked D'Oyly Carte if by any chance he was expecting to accommodate an amphibious clientele. Yet the remarkable fact is that the Victoria Hotel, *the* Savoy's *closest and most recent rival, provided only 4 bathrooms in an establishment catering for 500 guests.*

55 - *The Herzog Télesème (multiple telegraph) at the* Élysée Palace *hotel, Paris.*

56 - *Poster advertising the* Grand Hôtel, *Paris.*

57 and 58 - *The exterior and the Reading Room of the* Hôtel Terminus, *Paris //* The hotel was directly linked by footbridge to the arrival and departure platforms of Saint-Lazare Station. "There are three things one must be sparing of if one travels a lot: one's time, one's purse and one's fatigue. I get off the train and I have to get a cab to drag my luggage across town. I'll need another on departure to bring it all back. 5 or 6 francs soon go on cabs, tips, etc. But at Saint-Lazare I walk straight into the Hôtel Terminus, *giving my luggage chit to the porter, and already I'm in bed. On departure my ticket is brought to my room, my luggage registered without my having to leave the entrance hall. Amply warned I reach my compartment, in my slippers, directly by the footbridge. Thus I've saved time, money and trouble. Whereas I came once to Paris so now I'll come twice."* (From the brochure published for the opening of the hotel on the 7th of May, 1889.)

60

*Le grand Salon*
*Pera-Palace*

61

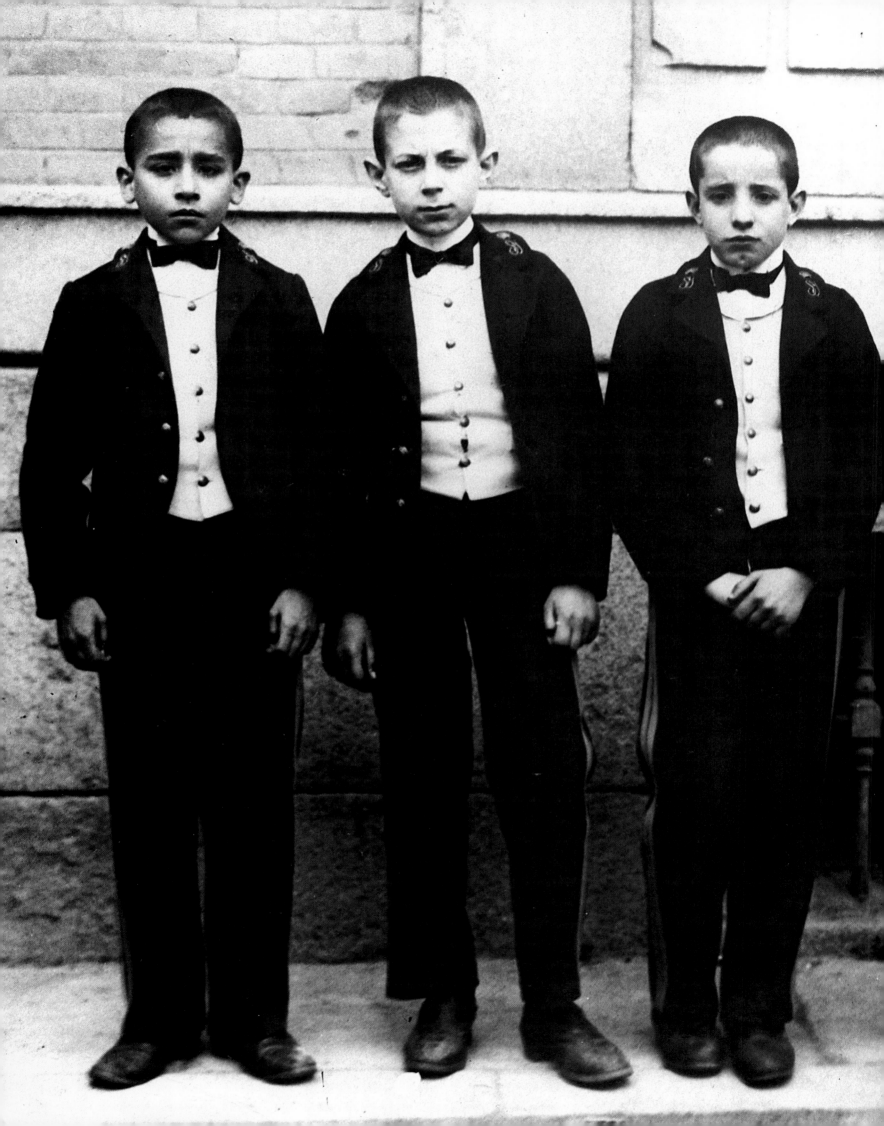

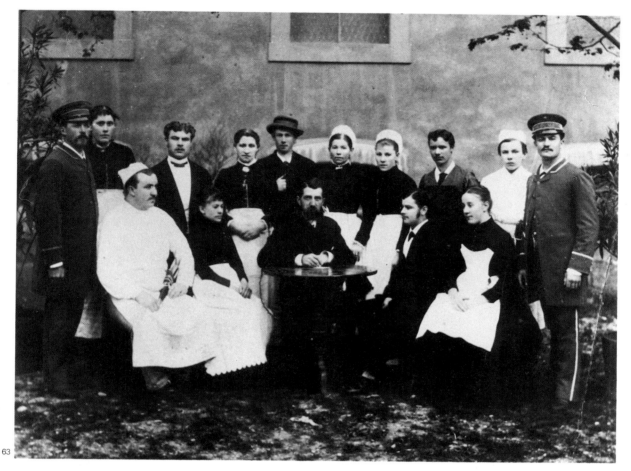

63

59 - *The Dining Room of the* Hôtel des Réservoirs, *Versailles, in an 1897 photograph.*
60 and 61 - *Drawing Room and Reading Room of the* Pera Palace, Istanbul // *Financed by Pullman's Palace Car Company, this hotel of 1892, catering for foreign tourists, was specifically European in design. One might have imagined oneself in London or Paris, but for the highly byzantine nonchalance of the staff evoked by Marcel Proust in "Within a Budding Grove": "Inside in the hall, the comrades of the (outside) page did not indeed work much harder than he did, but at least executed a few drilled movements. Probably in the early mornings they helped with the cleaning. But in the afternoons they just stood there like a Chorus who, even when there is nothing for them to do, remain on stage to strengthen the cast." It was in the* Pera Palace *that Agatha Christie wrote "Murder on the Orient Express".*
62 - *Three page boys // The hotel trade was a tough apprenticeship begun at an early age. On the other hand the prospects were limitless; with savoir faire there was always the chance of becoming a Monsieur Ritz or a Monsieur Negresco.*
63 - *The manager of the* Hôtel Richemond, Geneva, *surrounded by his staff (initially the* Richemont, *the name was for commercial reasons anglicized).* 64 - *The hotel omnibus // "Chère Madame, should God grant me life and health next year please would you keep my sunny little balcony covered with birds for me, my landscape of lake and greenery and, above all, keep the good your so delicately efficacious presence has done me. Keep my holidays at the Richemond for me". Letter from Colette to Madame Armleder (from the Visitors Book of the* Hôtel Richemond *which opened in 1875).*

62          64

65 and 66 - *The entrance hall and the chimney-piece of a reception room in the Hôtel Métropole, Brussels // In 1893, when the future Place de Brouckère was being formed, a family of brewers, the Wielemans, bought all the buildings of the Caisse d'Épargne (savings bank) and opened the Hôtel Métropole there in 1894. For the benefit of their principal patrons the hotel management commissioned a souvenir guide to Brussels in 1909. It vaunted the exotic beauties of the hotel's reception rooms, galleries and restaurant; here Renaissance style ceilings recalled the châteaux of the Loire; there lofty walls faced with the Tunisian marble "brèche de Numidie", in a style termed "a modern interpretation of the Romanesque" rubbed shoulders with Hindoo decoration. Everything was designed to please, to take one out of oneself, to surprise. The luxurious decor was combined with all the advantages of modern comfort: electric light, steam heating, a telephone service backed up by "copyists on the type writer" and above all a lift by Edoux, the Parisian company which had installed the Eiffel Tower lifts. All Europe rushed there.*

65    66

68

67   69

70

73

67 - *The* Hôtel Gallia, *Cannes* // *Opened in 1898, the hotel had 180 bedrooms and 6 tennis courts. In 1899, Sarah Bernhardt came here to perform "Froufrou" and "Phèdre".*

68 - *The first floor Drawing Room of the Ritz, Paris, retaining its late C.18th decoration.*

69 - *An early C.18th panelled study, adapted as a bathroom.*

70 - *Detail of late C.18th neo-classical door and panelling* // *The Hôtel de Grammont, built in 1704 behind Jules Hardouin-Mansart's earlier Place Vendôme façade, became the Hôtel Ritz in 1898. Preserving the dated charms of this old mansion, César Ritz, the hotel's founder, invented a complete life-style. Proust was unshakeable in his fidelity to the Ritz, indeed he was known as "Proust du Ritz": "There is nothing that amuses me less than what, twenty years ago now, was termed 'select'; what does amuse me are the social gatherings open to everyone that look like firework displays. A distraction I find at the Ritz". The Ritz became part of modern mythology, its name alone conjuring up elegance and refined luxury. In "Gentlemen Prefer Blonds" Marilyn Monroe has two criteria for making a good match — diamonds and the Ritz.*

71 - *The* Palace Regina Hôtel, *Nice* // *This hotel was built in 18 months, mobilizing a 4,000 strong work force. Queen Victoria regularly stayed at the Regina where a wing with a private lift was reserved for her.*

72 - *The* Hôtel du Palais d'Orsay, *Paris: the Reading Room* // *Architecturally an integral part of the Gare d'Orsay, the hotel opened for the World Fair of 1900. Its prosperity was closely linked with the importance of the station which was between the wars the main line terminus for Spain. The hotel then had 260 bedrooms and 4 grand reception rooms. Since it was built on the banks of the Seine, the precaution was taken to install the kitchens on the sixth floor, for the river regularly flooded the cellars. A speaking tube from the lower floors enabled orders to be passed to the kitchens. When the station was relegated to suburban line status, the hotel declined, finally closing in 1972.*

71

74

75

73 - *Receiving a guest at the turn of the century// The arrival of an important guest was the occasion for a fulldress ceremony involving a whole army of staff. More often than not the guests arrived by rail. The hotel had to telephone to check up on the times of trains. If a delay occured, the full complement of management and staff had to remain waiting whatever the hour. Carriages equal to the number of guests were sent off to the station, each one with a page boy who had to be on the platform to meet the guest. Countless and cumbersome pieces of luggage (40 items per couple was common) were taken up to the hotel in a separate vehicle. The average stay in one of these palaces was at least 15 days and often a month. Gentlemen were often accompanied by their valet, even their secretary, and ladies by their maid, while the chauffeur would join them with the car. The doorman would keep a lookout for arrivals and ring the bell as soon as he saw them, to warn the manager and head porter to be ready. After the customary welcome, the head porter would then see the guests to their rooms.*
74 and 75 - *The* Hotel Cecil, *London: the forecourt and the Barber's Saloon in 1911.*

# MENU

## NOZZE
### BODO - CAMPREDON D'ALBARETTO

5 Settembre 1908.

Potage reine de Poulet

Truite du Moncenis s.<sup>ce</sup> Cardinal

Filet de Bœuf au Printemps

Petits Pois au jambon

Faisan à la broche Cardés

Salade minuette

Glace à la crèole

Gâteau Marguerite

Friandises - Dessert

Demi tasse Moka

Capri blanc
Grignolino en caraffe
Barbaresco Calissano
Moët et Chandon frappè

**Grand Hôtel Turin**

LIT. BOERO

76 - *The Empire Style re-ception room of the* Hôtel de Paris, *Monte Carlo, with Paul Gervais's fresco, pain-ted in 1909, and the "Bac-chante with Roses" by Car-peaux// Set in the gardens of the Place du Casino, the* Hôtel de Paris *was opened in 1864, enlarged in 1865 and rebuilt in 1908 by Niermans.*

77 - *The restaurant of the* Savoy, *London. An adver-tisement of 1906// As soon as the hotel opened, the* Savoy's *restaurant became the smart rendez-vous. Eve-rything conspired for its suc-cess: César Ritz had been appointed manager and Escoffier the Chef. People from all over the world came to taste the famous "Pêche Melba" (named af-ter the Australian prima donna Nellie Melba) or the "Cuisses de nymphes à l'au-rore", the favorite dish of the Prince of Wales. Ritz's ultimate refinement was the idea that his patrons should dine to the strains of the waltz... and Johann Strauss was hired forthwith to conduct the orchestra. The experiment was a complete success; over-whelmed, the diners lingered at table, and of course the champagne flowed.*

78 - *Dining room of the* Ceres Pavilion *at the* Grand Hôtel, *Vit-tel// This grand hotel was built in 1912 on the site of a previous hotel (built in 1862, decorated by Garnier in 1884 and demolished in 1911). The Ceres Pavilion (erected in 1874, rebuilt in 1905) then became a wing of the new spa palace. The successive demolitions tell of a constantly developing ins-titution.*

79 - *A menu of the* Grand Hotel, *Turin, in 1908.*

80 - *An evening reception at the* Meurice *in Paris// In 1808, Mr. Meurice installed a coaching inn for the mail service to Calais, in the for-mer convent of the Feuil-lants. His clientele were the English, demanding guests whose fastidiousness in terms of comfort and service played a large part in the development of modern hotel standards. By fulfilling his guests' expectations, Mr. Meurice created one of the very first luxury hotels.*

81 - *Dinner on the terrace, painting by Paul Chabas.*

GRAND HOTEL

82

83

84

HOTEL
WEIMAR

BY APPOINTMENT

MARIENBAD.

HOFHOTELIER J. HAMMERSCHMIED.
EIGENTÜMER.

A.D.

EXCELSIOR HOTEL REGINA NICE......
...CIMIEZ.

# Grand Hôtel de l'Europe, Salzburg

Vergrössert und vollständig umgebaut nach den Ent-
würfen des Herrn Professor Dr. Max Fabiani, Wien.

**Appartements mit Privat-Bädern.**
45 HP.-Mercedes-Automobil.    **Abend-Konzerte.**

Prospekte auf Verlangen.

Unter persönlicher Leitung des Besitzers Georg Jung.

88

# HOTEL DE PARIS

HOTEL DE PARIS

# TROUVILLE S/MER

89

90

91

92

93

94

95

96

97

82 - *Dinner at the* Grand Hôtel, *Paris. Cartoon by Sem.*

83 - *Dinner at the* Ritz, *Paris.*

84 - *Dedication, dated 1902, by Alle Litoine, a famous performer of Wagner. From the visitor's book of the* Hôtel Métropole, *Brussels.*

85 - *Master pastry-cooks in a German grand hotel. Advertising pamphlets.*

86 - *The* Hotel Weimar, *Marienbad, opened in 1904.*

87 - Excelsior Hôtel Regina, *Nice.*

88 - *The* Grand Hotel de l'Europe, *Salzburg.*

89 - *Advertisement for the* Hôtel de Paris, *Trouville.*

90 - *The* Hotel Britannia, *Vienna (1872-1874).*

91 - *The* Hôtel de Paris, *Monte Carlo.*

92 - *The* Hotel Wohnaus Heinrichhof, *Vienna (1861-1863).*

93 - *The* Waldorf Hotel, *London (1906-1908).*

94 - *The* Hotel Furstenhof, *Bad Wildungen (1911).*

95 - *The* Caux Palace Hôtel, *Caux (1900-1902).*

96 - *The* Grand Hotel des Iles Borromées, *Stresa (1913).*

97 - *The* Hotel Goldener Löwe, *Reichenberg (1906).*

98 - *The* Grand Hotel Villa Igea, *Palermo: drawing room decorated with a fresco by E. De Maria Bergler // This hotel is one of the most significant works by the architect Ernesto Basile (1857-1932). If the principles and vocabulary of Art Nouveau make up the essence of his work, he interpreted these in an original manner. In particular he stressed the need to see the architectural work as a whole, integrating the building into its environment and closely relating its structural characteristics to its style. Looking out onto he sea, the Grand Hotel Villa Igea was completed in 1900. Since an already existing building was used, it was not possible to site the whole work ideally. Nevertheless, by the use of mirrors, transparency and contrasting colours, the marine luminosity was restored throughout.*

98

99

100

101

102

103

104

105

106

107

108

From the Second Empire
onward, gigantic scale and
ostentation become the
hallmarks of grand hotel
architecture. The grand hotel
is not only one of the
innovatory institutions of the
industrial age but a symbol,
a monument whose silhouette
crowns the letter headings
and publicity of the period.
Its ample façade is in itself
sufficient to proclaim the
hotel's merits and by
implication the merits of the
guests in residence. The
architectural vocabulary has
a conventional, indeed trite
elegance, aiming to convey
an instant illusion of
grandeur and solid
permanence. This "grand
hotel style" was to pervade
the whole of Europe, but in
such a happily eclectic
fashion that frequently
fantastical variety imposed
itself on the stereotype.
99 - The Hotel Esplana-
de// This hotel, one of the
largest in Berlin, was opened in 1908. As enlarged
and modernised in 1912 it
accommodated 400 guests.
100 - The Athénée Palace,
Bucharest.
101 - The Regina Palast,
Munich; built in 1908.
102 - The Montreux
Palace, Montreux; a 400
bedroom hotel built in 1908.

109

110

94

111

103 - *The* Grand Hôtel, *Cabourg; founded in 1862, enlarged and altered in 1881 and 1907.*
104 - *The* Montreux Palace: *the forecourt.*
105 - *The* Hôtel Majestic, *Nice: the forecourt; inaugurated in 1908.*
106 - *The* Hôtel du Palais, *Biarritz // Built as the "Villa Eugénie" for the Empress in 1854, converted to a hotel in 1894, it was enlarged and restored by Edouard Niermans in 1905.*
107 - *The* Hôtel Majestic, *Paris; inaugurated in 1905.*
108 - *The* Hotel Esplanade, *Berlin: courtyard façade.*
109 and 110 - *The* Montreux Palace: *the theatre, bar and billiard room.*
111 and 112 - *The* Hotel Esplanade, *Berlin: the entrance hall, the Palm Court. The exterior of a grand hotel is entirely intended to attract and inform the guest. Inside everything conspires to seduce, surprise and amaze him. Beyond the repetitive façades and past the reception, the hotel guest is 'king' and treated as such: sumptuous halls and saloons — a gigantic decor of contrasting styles and genres — provide the setting for his entertainment.*

112

95

115

116

117

118

119

120

121

118 - *The billiard tables in the* Hôtel du Palais, *Biarritz*. 119 - *The Tiger drawing room.* 120 - *The grand dining room.*
121 - *The American bar.*
122 - *A bedroom in the* Hôtel de Crillon, *Paris*.
123 - *A bedroom in the* Hôtel Meurice, *Paris*.
124 - *A bedroom in the* Hotel Adlon, *Berlin // Inaugurated in 1907, this hotel had 305 bedrooms.*
125 - *A bedroom in the* Hotel Esplanade, *Berlin. A direct competitor of the* Hotel Adlon, *the* Hotel Esplanade, *when it was converted in 1912, had only 102 bathrooms, whereas the* Adlon *could boast 140. On the other hand, all its bedrooms were equipped with telephones.*
*"The tinkling of crystal and silverware died away in the corridor and he was once more alone with his solitude. The steady reflection of the lighting in the tall mirrors made the bedroom larger; the room was too luminous, dilated, as it were, by the light which pervaded and suffused it and which mingled with the gold leafing of the frames, the brass inlaid furniture and the burnished gold mouldings on the ceiling and doors. And into the artificial silence procured by abundant hangings, heavy crystalware, layers of carpets and the portières, nevertheless there penetrated the shuddering restlessness of the town"* (Valery Larbaud – *200 Chambres, 200 Salles de Bains"*).

122

123

124

125

137

138

126 - *The* Hotel Adlon, *Berlin: monumental chimney-piece with, as overmantel, a bust of William II. This hotel, which cost no less than 17 million marks to build, was one of the most sumptuous in Germany. Its austere façade concealed a luxurious and highly refined interior decoration. It was destroyed during the war.*
127 - *The Palm Court of the* Hôtel Majestic, *Paris.*
128 - *The Louis XIV drawing room and the entrance to the restaurant.*
129 - *The outside restaurant.*
130 - *Anteroom of the grand suite.*
131 - *The Ladies Room.*
132 - *Bedroom.*
133 - *Bathroom in one of the suites.*
134 - *Bathroom, whose bath came from the former* Hôtel Basilewsky, *residence of Queen Isabel of Spain. The Majestic was built on the site of this residence.*
135 - *Bathroom in the Palace* Hôtel, *Madrid, built in 1910.*
136 - *Bathroom in the* Hôtel Esplanade, *Berlin.*
137-138 - *Bedrooms in the* Hôtel Majestic, *Nice, which opened on February 12th, 1908 // "Oh! I loved this hotel which was in the very centre of society. It is mentioned in the journal of a great 19th century foreign writer. He praises it, with one proviso - he found no soap in his bedroom. It was his first visit to the continent and he was unaware that people there were in the habit of choosing their own soap which they brought along with them in their luggage. They did not use any old soap. He was under the impression that they did not use soap in Europe. And he wrote so". (Valery Larbaud – "200 Chambres, 200 Salles de Bains").*

140

141

139 - *A hall in the* Hotel Meurice, *Paris*.
140 - *Rotunda in the* Ritz Hotel, London. 141 - *The Palm Court // The London* Ritz *was erected on the adjacent sites of the* Walsingham House Hotel *and the* Bath Hotel. *The building of the hotel was completed by the 1st of October 1905 and was described in the same year by the "Builders' Journal and Architectural Engineer" as being "the finest example in England of the use of American techniques". The innovative use of steel framing in particular attracted attention, along with the use of reinforced concrete, systematic fireproofing and the standardization of some of the material. For example, the granite for the façades, chosen for its colour and smooth surface, was Norwegian. The blocks were shipped from Norway, already cut and dressed to the required size and ready for use. Once more Mewès was called upon, the architect who had also designed in Paris both the Palais des Congrès (for the World Fair of 1900) and the interior architecture of the* Ritz *on the* Place Vendôme, *and in London had been responsible for the decoration of the* Carlton Hotel. *Here, breaking with the eclecticism of the previous decade, Mewès adopted a Louis XIV style throughout. When it was opened, the hotel had 150 bedrooms and reception rooms, 75 bathrooms. The decoration of the suites, in all its diversity, had been determined by an overall conception: white walls and paneling, pink and green Persian carpets on the floors.*

142

143

144

145

146

147

148

149

142 - *The* Hotel Metropole *(1899-1903), Moscow.*
143 - *The* Hotel Excelsior, *the Lido, Venice // Right from the beginning of C.20th, there were several attempts to make the Lido as a sea resort. However, and despite the opening of the* Hôtel des Bains *in 1901, this narrow strand was only frequented by Venetians and some artists and writers. The start of the real boom was due to a certain Nicolo Spada. This enterprising Venetian came up with the idea of erecting not precisely an hotel but rather a meeting place for the international elite. The local authorities did not favor this scheme – twice turned down – and thirteen plans were considered before the definitive project was settled upon. Nicolo Spada obtained financial backing from the Director of the Banco Commerciale in Venice who had among his collaborators Giuseppe Volpi, founder (in 1906) of the Ciga hotel chain. From 1908 the Ciga controlled all the hotels on the Lido. The Excelsior, lavishly inaugurated in 1907 as a venue for occasional society festivities, became a true hotel on the 20th of July 1908. It attracted a new, ultra-rich, cosmopolitan clientele, conspicuously furthering the fortunes of the Lido. In 1912, J.P. Morgan, the financier, exclaimed: "In America, everybody who has visited Europe is talking more about the Excelsior Palace than the Doge's Palace."*
144 - *The* Ritz Hotel, *London.*
145 - *The* Hôtel de Crillon, *Paris.*
146 - *The courtyard façade of the* Hotel Adlon, *Berlin.*
147 - *The* Excelsior Hotel Ernst, *Cologne.*
148 - *The* Hotel Excelsior, *Naples, opened in 1907.*
149 - *The* Hotel Astoria, *Petersburg, opened in 1908.*
150 - *The* Hotel Astoria, *Brussels // In 1909, the Mengelle boarding house became, on the initiative of its ambitious proprietor, the Hotel Astoria.*
151 - *The laying of the first stone of the* Palace Hotel, *Brussels, on the 28th of November, 1908.* 152 - *The façade of the hotel // The building of this seven storey hotel took less than eleven months.*

150

151

112

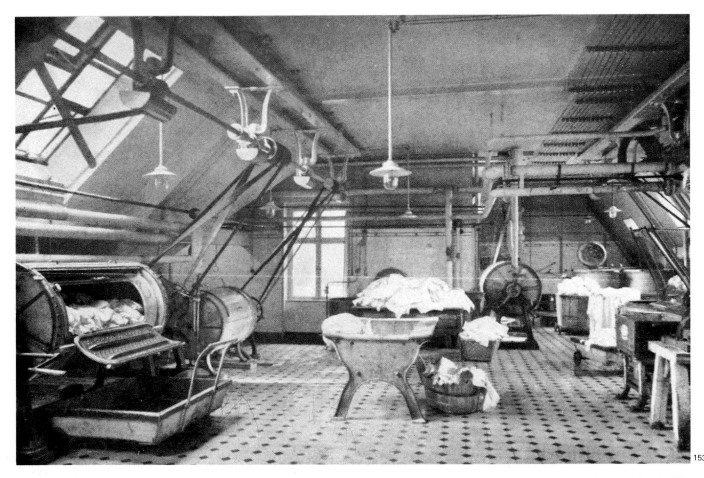

153

154

155

156

These palaces, which offered up an exterior image of resolute conformity, were in the forefront of technological advance before this was brought into the home. There is no innovation which they did not pioneer – running water, remote-controlled systems using flashing lights or ringing bells, electrical generators, rising mains, ventilation systems, central heating, etc. – all inventions which were elaborated in the grand hotels in order to improve the quality of service.

153 - The laundry in the Hotel Adlon, *Berlin, with its steam boilers and washing machines.*

154 - *Kitchens of the* Adelphi Hotel, *Liverpool, c. 1914.*

155 and 156 - *The wine cellar and bottling plant in the general store of the Ciga company.*

157 - *A team of cooks c.1900.*

158 - *The Master Pastry Cooks at the* Splendide Royal Hotel, *Lugano// C.1888, the "Villa Merlina", sited in a superb park opposite the lake, was converted, becoming the* Hotel Splendide, *with about 100 beds. In 1902 an annex was added: the "Villa Maria". In 1924 the establishment took on its definitive name of* Splendide Royal Hotel.

159 and 160 - *Receptionist, page-boys and coachmen (front and back) at the* Elysée Palace Hôtel, *Paris.*

"Still, if Françoise had associated only with the ladies' maids brought to the hotel by the other visitors ... no great harm would have been done ... But she had formed connections also with one of the wine-waiters, with a man in the kitchen, and with the head chambermaid of our landing. And the result of this in our everyday life was that ... since she had made friends with a personnage in the kitchen ... were my grandmother or I to complain of cold feet, Françoise, even at an hour that was quite normal, dared not ring; she assured us that it would give offence because they would have to light the furnace again, or because it would interrupt the servants' dinner and they would be annoyed ... So that it amounted to this, that we could no longer have any hot water because Françoise had become a friend of the man who would·have to heat it."
(Marcel Proust – "Within a Budding Grove")

157

158

116

159

160

DAVID

CARMEN.

Comment ne pas
aimer Bruxelles où
l'on vous accueille de
si gracieuse manière !
J'en garderai un
(1) un éternel souvenir
car j'y laisserai de
vrais amis.

*[signature]*

novembre 1905

(1) Dans mon emballement, j'ai biffé
le « un ». Excusez-moi, l'habitude !!!

162

163

120

3 Avril 1910

# REVUE DE LA
# *Riviera*
## Illustrée

**Revue hebdomadaire paraissant le Dimanche**

Robert COQUELLE, Rédacteur en Chef

Photos de MM. ENRIETTI, BENOIST
NAVELLO, etc., etc.

LES SOUVERAINS A MONTE-CARLO

S. A. R. GUSTAVE V, Roi de Suède, arrivant à l'Hôtel de Paris, sur Automobile Benz.

Photo NAVELLO

164

161 - *Dedication by the tenor David in the visitors' book of the* Hôtel Métropole, *Brussels* // *The memory of the grand hotels is tenuous. Some disappear leaving behind only a forgotten name and reputation, their archives scattered in the course of numerous rebuildings, conversions, changes of management, destroyed in fires or jumbled up in various requisitionings. The* Hôtel Métropole *has kept its memory intact: it's visitors' book, register and other documents were preserved for posterity. Great ironmasters such as Krupp, Schneider, Le Creusot, Cockerill, etc. would meet there; among it's guests: Georges Clemenceau, Marshall Foch, Sarah Bernhardt, Isadora Duncan, Jouvet, Strauss, Douglas Fairbanks, Raimu, Gide, Cocteau, Maurois and Sacha Guitry who, in 1932, referring to a previous stay of his, wrote in the visitors' book "1912! How time flies! 1932! If this page could be put aside just for my use, I'll sign it in 1952, 1972 and so on, every twenty years until 1985, my first centenary!" Nor has another exceedingly polite guest been forgotten. When the hotel was occupied by Wehrmacht officers, Field Marshal Goering used to collect his own key at the porter's desk so as not to trouble the night porter. The same Goering who showed no qualms about disturbing the slumber of little children in London.*

162 - *Clay pigeon shooting at the* Hotel Excelsior, *Lido, Venice.*

163 - *The orchestra of the* Hotel d'Angleterre, *Copenhagen, in 1908.*

164 - *The weekly chronicle of the "Revue de la Riviera".*

165 - *The* Midland Adelphi Hotel, *Liverpool, when it was rebuilt in 1911.* 166 and 167 - *The façade of the building completed in 1914 and the entry hall* // *The first Adelphi Hotel probably owed its success to Liverpool's becoming the main port of embarkation for America. In 1842, Charles Dickens, about to set off for the New World, stayed in this hotel and, it is said, highly appreciated the fare. A second building replaced the original in 1861 and became, from 1890, the property of the London Midland Co. A third and most recent building followed between 1911 and 1914.*

165

166  167

122

169

168    170

125

168 - *The caretaker at the* Midland Adelphi Hotel, *Liverpool.*
169 - *The Solvay council of physicists at the* Hôtel Métropole, *Brussels* // *In 1911, on the occasion of a scientific council, the* Métropole *was host to Planck, Lorentz, Einstein, Marie Curie, Langevin, Rutherford, de Broglie and other scientists of international repute. Here we see them all gathered for the official photo. The candles on the table are a reminder that, in 1911, electricity was still in its uncertain infancy.*
170 - *In the Palm Court of the* Hotel d'Angleterre, *Copenhagen, an evening reception in honor of the Norwegian explorer Roald Amundsen, the first man to reach the South Pole.*
171 *and* 172 - *The outside hall and the Palm Court of the* Palace Hotel, *Madrid.*
173 - *Fresco — by Gerveix — and the main hall in the* Hôtel Négresco, *Nice* // *Henri Négresco, born in Bucharest in 1868, left his native Rumania when he was fifteen. He travelled throughout Europe, working his way up through all the steps of a hotel career before he thought of creating, in Nice, the future Hôtel Négresco. Completed in 1912, the building was the work of one of the greatest hotel architects of the time, Edouard Niermans. This Dutch architect, an innovator of Art Nouveau, restored the* Hôtel du Palais, *in Biarritz, and designed, among others, the* Hôtel de Paris, *in Monte Carlo, the* Savoy, *in Fontainebleau, the* Palace Hotel, *in Madrid (opposite) and the* Palace Hôtel, *Ostend. He is also responsible for some of the hallowed "night spots" of Paris such as the Folies-Bergère and the Casino de Paris.*

171

172

173

174

175

174 - *The* Grosvenor Hotel, *London: the hall* // *This hotel, completed c.1910, was built near the new Victoria Station by the London, Brighton and South Coast Railway Company.*
175 - *The dining room in the* Grand Hotel, *Northumberland Avenue, London, opened in 1881* // *The restaurant was open to both guests and non-residents.*
176 - *The dining room in the* Grand Hôtel, *Vittel, built in 1912 by Georges Walwein on the site of the earlier hotel of 1862.*
*"I could be seen in the dining hall, assisted by an imbecile, preparing six tables for luncheon, spreading damask cloths over the soft base pads, setting places and, from twelve-o-clock on, pencil in hand, taking down order of those who had come. Bowing, one hand behind my back in the best waiters' tradition, I would proffer the dishes; now and then I would practise the fine art of manipulating fork and spoon with my right hand alone, to serve those who preferred me to do it for them". (Thomas Mann – "The Confessions of Felix Krull, Confidence Man.")*

176

129

177

178

179

81

82

177 - *The* Hôtel Lutetia, *Paris : at the foot of the main hall, balcony forming a gallery and housing a fountain.* 179 - *The façade of the hotel // The hotel with its 200 bedrooms and bathrooms was built in two stages: the main building — completed in 1910 — is the work of Tauzin and Boileau. The latter architect completed the building with an annex inaugurated in 1912. "The statuary lends to the whole of the façade an element of delight, peculiarly French, drawing its motifs from one of our national treasures, the vine, everywhere adorning the projections of the building and climbing to the very top of its highest gables." (Henri Tauzin — "L'Architecte" 1911.)*

178 - *The Palm Court of the* Hôtel Bellevue, *Bern // The former* Bellevue *built in 1865 stood until 1911. The new building was completed in 1913.*

180, 181 and 182 - *Storerooms in the main store of the Ciga hotel chain, Venice.*

183 - *Theatre in the* Hotel Cecil, *London.*

184 - *Small theatre in the* Hotel Excelsior, *Lido, Venice.*

185 - *The "terrasse" of the* Palace Hôtel, *St.-Moritz // The story goes that it was in September 1864 that Johannes Badrutt, the proprietor of what was still then the Hôtel Kulm, invented winter sports. For a bet, he proposed to four Englishmen who had been staying with him, and who were on the eve of their departure, that they stay on, all expenses paid, until the spring "so that they might, for once in their lives, take advantage of a superb, sunny winter". The Englishmen, quite naturally, took him up on it, staying on until March and, delighted, came back with their families and friends. Badrutt's Palace Hôtel was built in 1895, two storeys being added in 1907. In 1911, an adjoining restaurant and Europe's very first covered tennis court were built.*

186 - *In the* Hotel Excelsior's *private gondola, Lido, Venice.*

183

184

134

185

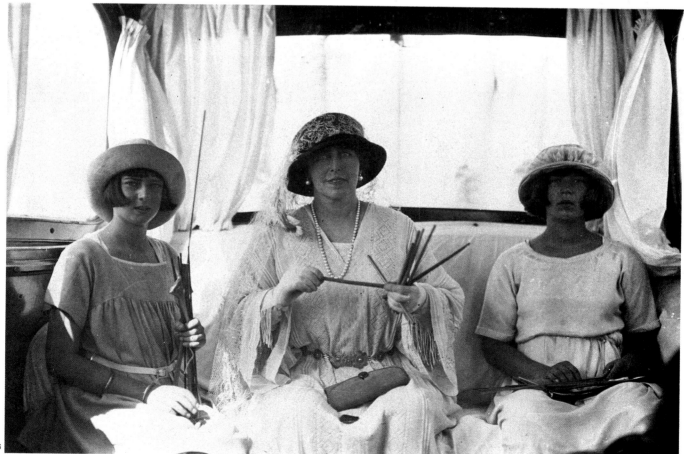

186

135

EXCELSIOR
PALACE HOTEL
VENISE-LIDO
GRAND ETABLISSEMENT DE BAINS-CASINO-KURSAAL
PONTE
DELLA FENICE

188

189

Bombardment of Scarborough by the German Fleet. Dec. 16th 1914.
The Grand Hotel.
3638.

190

191

192

193

194

140

195

187 - *On the walls of Venice, a poster advertising the* Hotel Excelsior.
188 - *The Bey of Tunis, on a visit to Paris, staying at the* Hôtel Meurice.
189 - *The* Hôtel Négresco, *Nice, transformed into a military hospital in September 1914. The second person, top left, is Mr. Négresco who was to find himself practically ruined at the end of the war.*
190 - *The* Grand Hotel, *Scarborough, shelled by the German navy on the 16th December 1914.*
191 - *Dressing station on the first floor of the* Hôtel Astoria, *Paris, converted into a Japanese hospital in 1915.*
192 - *The* Hôtel Meurice: *grand charity sale in aid of the wounded, in January 1917.*
193 - *The King of Montenegro leaving the* Meurice *for the* Elysée, *July 29th 1916.*
194 - *Lloyd George leaving the* Hôtel de Crillon *which, during both World Wars, housed the allied general staff.*
195 - *English soldiers billeted in the* Trianon Palace, *Versailles.*
196 - *Requisition of the* Hôtel Impérial, *Frankfurt.*

196

141

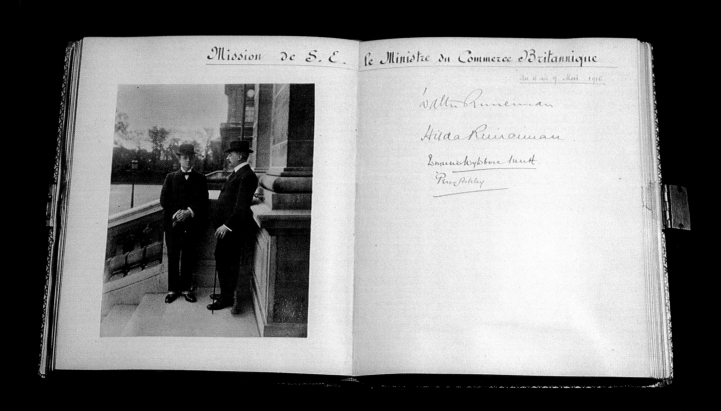

du 4 au 9 Mai 1916

Walter Runciman

Hilda Runciman

Emma Wyndham Hunt

Peter Ashley

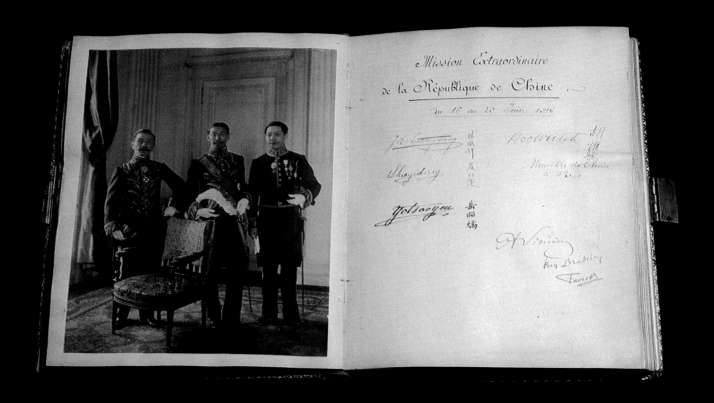

Mission Extraordinaire
de la République de Chine
du 16 au 20 Juin 1914

199

200

197 and 198 - *Extracts from the* Hôtel de Crillon's *visitor's book: mission of His Excellency, the President of the Board of Trade and the special mission of the Republic of China // Only a stone's throw from the Champs Elysées, scene both of France's victory parades and her public mourning, the* Hôtel de Crillon *was no mere a leisure resort. From the day of its opening it constantly thronged with kings, princes, statesmen, ministers and diplomats from the four corners of the earth. At the end of World War I, it was in the* Crillon, *in 1919, that sat the commission, appointed by the preliminary peace conference with a view to working out the constitution and role of a League of Nations, forerunner of the UNO. In other words, the* Crillon *has traditionally played a semi-official role and the guests of the Elysée were often its guests.*

199 and 200 - *It was in the present-day dining room of the* Trianon Palace, *Versailles, that in 1920, by the treaty of Trianon, the victorious powers settled the fate of Hungary.*

201 - *The gardens of the* Palasthotel Quellenhof – *today the* Parkhotel Quellenhof, *Aix-la-Chapelle. This hydropathic establishment was built in 1916.*

202 - *Palm Court of the* Hotel Excelsior, *Lido, Venice.*

203 - *The "terrasse" of the* Metropole Hotel, *Brighton // This hotel, opened in 1890, quickly outshined its neighbor, the* Grand Hotel, *in business since 1864. The* Metropole *gained excellent publicity from being the last stage of the famous London-Brighton car rally.*

202

203

# A HOMAGE TO CESAR RITZ

## HUGH MONTGOMERY-MASSINGBERD

E ffecting an entry through the revolving doors into one of the palace hotels that have survived more or less intact can still be an experience to elevate the most travel and care-worn spirits.

There is something intoxicatingly theatrical about the best of these places which can transform the dowdiest duckling into a swan. Stage fright, sometimes induced by stuffy, snobbish, and second-rate establishments, should not rear its head at palace hotels, the greatest of which have always generated an unobtrusively friendly and welcoming atmosphere. The tone is set from the start with the smooth removal of luggage, the minimum of fuss over registration at the reception desk, and, above all, the immediate sense of belonging. The guest may be flattering himself, but he feels at home in this fantasy world—and he is encouraged to do so. On his second visit he will be left in no doubt that his is a familiar face. What distinguishes the great palace hotels from other equally (or often even more) expensive hotels is not only the noble proportions of the architecture, the beauty of the interior decoration, the unsparing quality of the fittings, and the staff's unfailing personal attention to detail, but also that elusive commodity—style.

Every palace hotel has had its own style, its own special ambience, but there is no denying a general debt to the greatest of hoteliers, César Ritz, whose career was so closely linked with the immortal chef Auguste Escoffier. Bernard Berenson aptly dubbed the luxuriant kingdom of palace hotels "Ritzonia".

In 1870, where our story begins, Ritz, the twenty-year-old son of an Alpine smallholder, was working as a waiter at the Voisin Restaurant in Paris, when "elephant trunk, sauce chasseur" had to be added to the menu during the desperate siege of the city by the Prussians. After the Franco-Prussian War, the rich Americans—like the Vanderbilts, Morgans, Goulds, and other merchant princes—began to arrive in Europe in large numbers. Now the new palace hotels would become the melting pots for a cosmopolitan society.

Ritz shrewdly noted the needs and tastes of both the "old" and the "new" groups, whether it was ice-water for the Americans or Egyptian cigarettes for Albert Edward, Prince of Wales. The great hotelier banned heavy furnishing materials in favour of washable fabrics, and replaced wallpaper with paint. He was the pioneer of hotel bedrooms each having its own bathroom. In *César Ritz : Host to the*

*César Ritz.*
*Left page:*
*entrance of*
*the Hôtel Ritz,*
*place Vendôme,*
*Paris.*

*World* his widow asserted that Ritz "was one of the greatest civilizing influences of his time as regards this point of hygiene and sanitation" a claim that is by no means fanciful.

At the age of twenty-seven, Ritz became the manager of the Grand Hotel National at Lucerne and made it the most elegant hotel in Europe. In the early 1880s, as Mme Ritz recorded, "great ladies such as the Duchesse de La Rochefoucauld, the Duchesse de Maille, the Comtesse Greffulhe, Lady Leche, Lady Greville, the Duchess of Leeds, and the Duchess of Devonshire actually appeared in the public ballrooms and dining room and lent their enthusiastic support to the special fêtes there which Ritz organized". At the Grand Hotel in Monte-Carlo, Ritz joined forces with Escoffier to develop their ideas of what a luxury hotel should be. The emphasis was to be on comfort, cuisine, and service, since both men had a passion for cleanliness and order. From the 1880s onwards the two geniuses worked in tandem, civilizing hotels all over Europe.

In 1888, when Ritz was running the Hotel de Provence in Cannes, he received an offer he could not refuse from the impresario Richard D'Oyly Carte, whose Savoy Hotel overlooking the Thames in London was nearing completion. "He wants the *clientèle* I can give him", Ritz noted in his diary, "the people who come here, who go to Baden, who were my patrons at Lucerne and Monte-Carlo : the Marlborough House set—Lord Rosebery, Lord and Lady Elcho, Lord and Lady Gosford, Lord and Lady de Grey, and the Sassoons, the Roman princes, Rudini, the Crespis, the Rospigliosis, the Radziwills, and so forth ; the best of the theatre and opera crowd—Patti, the De Reszkes, Coquelin, Bernhardt ; the Grand Dukes and the smart Parisian crowd—the Castellanes, the Breteuils, the Sagans ; he wants the Vanderbilts and Morgans; he wants the Rothschilds. He wants to make his hotel the Hotel de luxe of London and of the world". And thanks to Ritz and Escoffier, D'Oyly Carte got what he wanted. Previously it had not been at all the form to eat in a public restaurant, but Ritz managed to bring about a significant change in the pattern of London life whereby dining out at the Savoy became a fashionable pursuit.

He was to do the same for the more formal Paris in the exquisitely elegant hotel named after him in the Place Vendôme, which opened in 1898. Ritz's triumph was complete when the genial Boni de Castellane, whose vast dinner parties were legendary for having the same number of footmen as guests, accosted him after dining at the hotel. "I'm going to dismiss my *chef*", said the Marquis to the hotelier. "It's foolish to try to compete with you and Escoffier". On one occasion, in the early years of the Paris Ritz, Castellane brought along his aunt, Princess Antoine Radziwill, to dine—somewhat against the aged *grande dame's* better inclinations. When she returned to Berlin, the Princess wrote to her nephew : "And I did think it so amusing, that time you took me to dine at the *inn*".

Recalling the opening of the Paris Ritz, Mme Ritz asserts that "it would be quite impossible to list completely the princes, financiers, great hostesses, beauties, sportsmen, writers, artists, famous connoisseurs and *gourmets*, dictators of fashion and rulers of the world's destinies, who thronged the great reception rooms". Henry Higgins, one of his backers, told César : "Kings and Princes will be jealous of you, Ritz. And they will copy you. You are going to teach the world how to live".

Ritz's greatest patron, the Prince of Wales (later King Edward VII), who once declared "Where Ritz goes, I go", duly transferred his Parisian custom from the long-established Hotel Bristol to the new Ritz. The Carlton Hotel in London, Ritz's next venture, was given Louis XVI interiors especially designed to appeal to the Prince who dined publicly in the restaurant.

Unfortunately the shock caused by the postponement of Edward VII's Coronation (due to the new King's peritonitis) in the summer of 1902 precipitated a nervous breakdown from which Ritz never fully recovered. Although he was not to die until 1918 (in a sanatorium in his native Switzerland), the "king of hoteliers" had only a nominal connection with the London Ritz, the Madrid Ritz, and the other hotels round the world that were to make his surname universally synonymous with elegance, *chic*, and luxury.

Happily, Ritz left a band of disciples determined that the immaculate standards of food, service, and décor associated with his name would not be lowered. Indeed, the London Ritz represents perhaps the supreme consummation of his genius, although it did not open until 1906, by which time Ritz was a shadow of the former self who had spent hours choosing the lampshades of exactly the right shade of pink to set off the complexions of his lady guests. There are those who have questioned the Ritzian "legend", and much is made of his virtual dismissal from the Savoy. Certainly his widow's extravagantly absurd memoirs, although delightful, cannot entirely be reelied upon, and many of his contemporaries in the hotel business thought Ritz was too pushy by half. "Many people imagine that Ritz invented the French menu, almost the French cuisine", grumbled W.J. Wilson of the vast Hotel Cecil, which was next door to the Savoy. "Instead of which he was an excellent imitator and propagandist from his youth up, and... made every Swiss

*Auguste Escoffier.*

*Right page :*
*Ballroom and jazzband at the* Savoy *Hotel, London.*

waiter believe there was the baton of a *maître d'hôtel* in every serviette". However, the fact remains that many things we now envisage as being part and parcel of a palace hotel originated with César Ritz. As we saw in the first chapter, the organization of the main circulation spaces of an hotel around a palm court originated with him, and he would plan the interiors so as to enable ladies to make dramatic entrances.

In theatrical terms, Ritz was a showman, a brilliant director and producer, who set the stage for the star performances by the *clientèle*. For without these players it would have been a dumb show and, in practical terms, a costly flop. The fascination with palace hotels has as much to do with the figures who gave the establishments their distinctive style as with their architectural and technical background. For the nostalgic, the palace hotel provides an irresistible feast of anecdotal associations. There, in Rome's Grand Hotel, Émile Zola burrowed under the sheets during a thunderstorm while here, at the Ritz, Marcel Proust stood on the balcony to watch the Gotha air raid on Paris in July 1917.

"The Duke and Duchess of Lancaster" (the travelling *noms de plume* of King Edward VII and Queen Alexandra) patronized the Paris Ritz "incognito", and it could be said, without becoming too carried away, that César Ritz played a part in the *Entente Cordiale* achieved by the underrated diplomatist-King. Meanwhile Mme Ritz recalled that during his visit to the hotel in 1907, the King "for no reason we could grasp... had a certain piece of rather intimate plumbing altered to suit him". The Paris Ritz also featured in the sordid saga of the socialist Countess of Warwick's attempt to blackmail the royal family over her affair with Edward VII. For it was in the suite of the royal "go-between" Arthur Du Cros, MP, that Lady Warwick and her "agent", the notorious scoundrel Frank Harris, met to thrash out their piece of business concerned with the letters from King Edward that began "My darling Daisy...".

The London Ritz's most celebrated royal resident was King Zog of the Albanians, who arrived in 1940 with a formidable retinue of bodyguards. Some of the large amounts of the royal luggage seemed exceptionally heavy, and George, the Ritz's hall porter, asked His Majesty if they contained anything of great value. "Yes", said King Zog, "gold". In as much as the King preferred something more exclusive than the hotel's air-raid shelter, the Ritz obligingly converted the ladies' cloakroom for the Albanian's use as a private shelter. Another larger-than-life royal personage to feature prominently in the history of the London Ritz was that giant of the Turf, the late Aga Khan, who kept a permanent suite for over forty years and entertained the unlikely figure of Mahatma Gandhi (in his loincloth) at this sybaritic hotel in 1931 during the Round Table Conference on India. The Aga used to breakfast off green figs and mangoes, which had to be shipped specially to him.

The essayist Peregrine Worsthorne spoke for many when he wrote of feeding at the London Ritz "not on oysters and champagne, but on memories of a past world". Such memories can be broadly divided into the two vintages of the palace hotel : the decade-and-a-half before the First World War and the decade afterwards.

*La belle époque*, that opulent and overblown period from the late-1890s to 1914, saw the fusion of the grand old world with the rich new world in a festival of frivolity and fun. An interchangeable cosmopolitan "society" could be found drifting through palace hotels in London, Paris, Cannes, Monte-Carlo, Vienna, Marienbad, and Biarritz (the latter's popularity possibly even owing something to the magical last syllable "ritz" !). Hand in hand with the full flowering of the palace hotel went the burgeoning of the great transatlantic liner, ferrying in the American *clientèle*. It was the age of elegant aristocratic wits such as Robert de Montesquiou and Boni de Castellane (who married the American railroad heiress, Anna Gould), as well as of *les grandes horizontales*, like Liane de Pougy and "La Belle Otéro" from the *demi-monde*. By the turn of the century *le Tout Paris* was certainly no longer confined to the native French, for the Parisian palace hotels had now been invaded by the more worldly Americans. The ranks of the rich in Britain were likewise swelled by families of foreign origin : American, South African, Greek, German-Jewish.

The court chamberlain of the *avant-guerre* world at the Paris Ritz was the legendary Olivier Dabescat, the monocled maître d'hôtel who sorted out sheep from goat among the big spenders. Olivier would stand no nonsense from the likes of James Gordon Bennett, the eccentric American newspaper proprietor, even though his income was said to be one million after tax. Bennett had a distressing tendency to behave in a violent and unpredictable manner, prompting his fellow American, the *boulevardier* Lucius Beebe, to observe that somebody who might conceivably fall down in the middle of the Ritz dining room and start chewing the carpet rated no special consideration from the haughty Olivier. Once Bennett got into a glass-smashing mood, Olivier would suggest that the action was brisk that night at Maxim's.

"I have given Monsieur the best table", Olivier would say a dozen times each evening, whenever a favourite client entered. In a long career Olivier's preferred clients included such royal personages as the Prince of Wales (later, briefly, Edward VIII and then Duke of Windsor), Alfonso of Spain, Manoel of Portugal, and the Shah of Persia, although after the Russian Revolution the great maître d'hôtel remarked with disdain of poor Grand Duke Boris : "that sort only drinks beer nowadays". At the same time Olivier was not averse to piloting the obese, overpainted, but immensely rich widow of John Mackay, the Bonanza King of the Comstock, to a choice table beside, say, the Duc de Gramont. In his time, too, Olivier was to strategically place the Dolly Sisters at a table midway between Mrs. Stuyvesant Fish and that engaging eccentric Berry Wall, who invariably dined with his chow dog. The chow was suitably attired in an ornate dinner jacket ; his stock collars and old-fashioned black satin stock ties made by Charvet from the same pattern as his master's.

Olivier was as solicitous to the dog's needs as he was to the green-eyelidded Marquise Cassatti's boa constrictor, which favoured a diet of live rabbits; and to Mrs. McLean's hooded falcon, which had a taste for live pigeons. With a straight face, Olivier asked Mrs. McLean whether the bird of prey preferred any particular breed of pigeon. On Christmas Day 1900, another whimsical American decided to challenge Olivier's claim that he could supply anything his clients might order and asked for elephant's feet (shades of the Siege of Paris). The resourceful maître d'hôtel duly bought an elephant from the Jardin des Plantes (Paris's Zoo) and served up the four feet to the eccentric's party. Olivier also kept back a small portion for Calouste Gulbenkian's table, where the oil magnate's four-year-old son, Nubar, was watching, eyes agog. "I was given a small mouthful", recalled Gulbenkian junior in his autobiography *Pantaraxia*, "it tasted like something between sponge and flanelette". Later in life the expansive Nubar was to be found in the kitchens of the Carlton Hotel at Cannes making sure that the *hure de sanglier truffé aux pistaches* ("truffled boar's head with pistachios") was prepared to his satisfaction.

Harold Nicolson, the diarist, had a very high opinion of Olivier of the Ritz, praising the way he blended with "a masterly precision the servile and the protective, the deferential and the condescending". But on one occasion, as Nicolson bore painful witness, Olivier's phenomenal memory failed him. The young diplomat agreed to lunch with the couturier Captain Edward Molyneux, whom he had met in the Rue de Rivoli, provided, said Nicolson, "we go to the Ritz. Olivier is the only head waiter who knows me, and I enjoy that". They duly filed into the dining room of the Ritz, where Olivier greeted Molyneux *(Bonjour, mon capitaine. Comment allez-vous ?)*, but all he could find to say to Nicolson was "Mr. Bonstetten is it not ?" Molyneux observed to his guest that he had never seen a man so gratuitously make himself look foolish.

Olivier was the model for Antoine, the central character in Édouard Bourdet's play *Le Sexe faible*, first produced in 1929 and set in a grand hotel. There is also more than a little of Olivier in Aimé, the head waiter of the Grand Hotel at Balbec in, perhaps, the greatest novel of this cen-

tury, *A La Recherche du temps perdu*, whose author, Marcel Proust, the chronicler of *la belle époque*, is forever associated with the Paris Ritz. "For Proust", thought the Duchesse de Clermont-Tonnerre, "Olivier was a kind of chief of secret police, and replaced Montesquiou as an informer".

George Painter, Proust's masterly biographer, has recorded that "Proust of the Ritz" found a second home in the hotel, "a substitute for the palaces of Cabourg, Venice and Evian which he would never see again.... At the Ritz he found again the movement and enigmas of a miniature world, the comfort and security of family life, the satisfaction of his lifelong craving for reciprocal service and gratitude". Proust himself summed up the atmosphere of the Ritz—and, in a way, great palace hotels—for all time, when he said: "They don't hustle me, and I feel at home here".

Lady Diana Cooper, the legendary beauty and ageless survivor from *la belle époque*, recalls the all-too-brief period before the First World War as the real "heyday of the Ritz in London". It was, she recalls, the first hotel to which young unmarried women were allowed to go unchaperoned. "My mother would not let me go to hotels", continues Lady Diana. "Not the Carlton... but that didn't matter, it was really an hotel for men anyway; certainly *not* the Savoy—that was where men took ladies. The Ritz, however, was different". Her mother, the Duchess of Rutland, liked beauty, and in her eyes the London Ritz was "beautiful, a palace". As a young girl, Lady Diana lived near the present site of the London Ritz several years before the hotel was even built; yet in 1984 she was over in Paris being interviewed on French television at the Hotel Meurice.

Nor would Lady Diana's mother have approved of the setup on the Riviera where the *demi-mondaines* held sway at the Hotel de Paris in Monte-Carlo. Here, as Christopher Matthew tells us in *A Different World : Stories of Grand Hotels*, Liane de Pougy trumped Otéro with jewellery that outshone her rival by placing it on her own maid. At the suggestion of Grand Duke Michael, the Carlton at Cannes ushered in the modern world when it instituted a mixed bar and had it launched by Mrs. William Leeds (later Princess Christopher of Greece). Here Charlie Forrester, the barman, taught the future Marchioness of Milford Haven and her sister, the future Lady Zia Wernher, how to use a cocktail shaker.

The Jazz Age decade, between the United States Congress's passage of prohibition in 1919 and Wall Street's Black Friday of 1929, was the next climactic moment for the palace hotel. Life took on a more frenetic pace in the wake of a war that had wasted the golden Edwardian generation. It was the age of the "American in Paris", and the new American-style bars established at the Ritz, the Crillon, and other palace hotels came to represent the era in all its raffish glory. Lucius Beebe has described how King Alfonso of Spain, accompanied by his friend the "King of the Dudes", Berry Wall, would come in for a drink known in His Majesty's absence as "King's Death" but called a "Royal Highball" when the monarch was present. It consisted of a quart of ice-cold champagne served in a large glass with a generous slug of vintage cognac and a handful of fresh strawberries. The Ritz Bar became a focal point for Paris visitors.

Scott Fitzgerald used the Ritz in several of his stories (although in fact *A Diamond as Big as the Ritz* related to the Ritz-Carlton in New York) and introduced his less famous compatriot Ernest Hemingway, then a beardless and equally moneyless loafer on the Left Bank, to the Ritz Bar. Hemingway would later brag of how he "liberated" the Ritz from the Nazis in 1944 and of his dream of the afterlife. "The action", he said, "always takes place in the Paris Ritz. It's a fine summer night. I knock back a couple of martinis in the bar, Cambon side. Then there's a wonderful dinner under a flowering chestnut tree in what's called *Le Petit Jardin*. That's the little garden that faces the Grill. After a few brandies I wander up to my room and slip into one of those huge Ritz beds. They are all made of brass. There's a bolster for my head the size of the Graf Zeppelin and four square pillows filled with real goose feathers—two for me and two for my quite heavenly companion".

"Ritzonia" at this time evokes images of a cast containing many famous "Twenties" figures. Michael Arlen, author of *The Green Hat* and once introduced by the hostess Lady Cunard as "the only Armenian who has not been massacred", garnered his copy at the London Ritz and the Savoy. Lorelei Lee, Anita Loos's heroine from Little Rock, moved from one Ritz Hotel to another, pronouncing them "devine" in the classic novel *Gentlemen Prefer Blondes*. Noël Coward was inspired to write the song "Children of the Ritz" by the sight of Barbara Hutton's finger nails tipped with mother-of-pearl, and based "I went to a Marvellous Party" on the Riviera exploits of the indefatigable Elsa Maxwell. This extraordinary female once sang some of Cole Porter's "secret" songs at a party given by the interior decorator Elsie de Wolfe (Lady Mendl) for Arthur Balfour, and then proceeded to arrange an elaborate dinner party at the Paris Ritz for the bemused British politician. It was at a corner table of the Ritz Bar that Porter wrote:

> *The world admits*
> *Even bears in pits do it—*
> *Even pekineses in the Ritz do it.*
> *Let's do it, let's fall in love.*

In Paris the Hollywood film stars flocked to the new Hotel George V, and in London the new Dorchester proved equally popular. After Charlie Chaplin was mobbed at the London Ritz in 1921, the hotel tended to keep film stars at bay, but the Savoy, with its own press office, has always been more geared to "showbusiness", in its various guises from Gilbert and Sullivan, Oscar Wilde, Lillie Langtry, and Nellie Melba to George Gershwin, Tallulah Bankhead, and Ivor Novello.

Vicky Baum's Grand Hotel, another famous fictional story about the escapist world of "Ritzonia", also appeared in 1929. Later filmed with Greta Garbo, it is supposedly based on the Hotel Adlon in Berlin, which was to suffer a fate worse than death at the hands of the East Berlin authorities, who, in the words of Hedda Adlon, used it "as a sort of overnight hostel for State employees". Making our exit, we bring the curtain down on the last line of Grand Hotel: "The revolving door turns and turns—and swings... and swings... and swings..."

*The "terrasse" restaurant at the* Hôtel Ritz, Paris.

# POMP AND CIRCUMSTANCE

## PIERRE-JEAN RÉMY

Once upon a time there were palaces, châteaux, and gardens, all with follies. Princes and Emperors—even a minor Marquis or two—received their guests at home, and a Fouquet could, in honour of Louix XIV, throw such an extravagant party at Vaux-le-Vicomte that it caused not only wigs but actual crowns to totter. Soon thereafter, the overreaching Finance Minister found himself in jail. After all, the sovereign's servant was not supposed to outshine the Sun King himself !

Then, there was Venice, where during Carnival every palace became the theatrical setting for a masked ball, which flowed into the streets, filling the town with masques and bergamasques. People mixed and mingled from palace to palace, drinking, eating, making love, simply parading, and, when necessary, reshaping history between minuets.

The festivities even produced opera. In 1629, for the wedding of Giustiniana Mocenigo and Lorenzo Giustiniani at the Palazzo Dandolo, two steps away from the Doges' Palace, Strozzi wrote *The Abduction of Proserpine*, fourteen years before Monteverdi's *Coronation of Poppea*, generally considered to be the first opera. But what a curious prelude to a honeymoon !

Palaces, châteaux, follies—all were products of a time when fêtes and high politics went hand in hand. Some palaces were even put up for just that purpose, among them the Villa Eugénie, built in Biarritz at the height of the Second Empire as a place where Napoleon III and the Empress Eugénie could spend the summer cooled by ocean breezes. While affairs of state took precedence in the small salons, fed by dossiers brought down from Paris by a member of the cabinet, the Imperial household continued their life in the grand salons, there formulating a style shaped by Charles Garnier and known as Second Empire. As the Empress busied herself organizing *tableaux vivants*, her husband took care of visiting Ambassadors. At dusk, everybody regrouped for a ball and fireworks in honour of such illustrious guests as the King of Württemberg or the King of the Belgians. Whenever protocol or propriety dictated, as during the mourning period for a Spanish Queen, the court waltzed in black. Parties and history, politics and love affairs, those who chronicled the one or the other found themselves crossing paths at regular intervals under the coffered ceilings of royal Europe. All this was just yesterday, or perhaps the day before.

Meanwhile, times have changed. After so much dancing under the gilded coffers, the crowns finally had one waltz too many, and,

*Dom Pedro, Emperor of Brazil, and his family in 1890, staying at the Brenner's Park Hotel, Baden-Baden, called in those days the "Villa Stéphanie". Left page : "Le Bal", by J. Tissot.*

one by one, they rolled into the warehouse of history's discards. Wars and revolutions did away with the rest, leaving the palaces and châteaux to become museums or vacation colonies. Those still able to keep them up had so many ceilings to regild that little was left for balls. Furthermore, the new heads of state and their Ambassadors had no stomach for discussing tomorrow's peace in the grand gallery of a once and futureless King. Of course, there were the treaties of Versailles, Sèvres, and Trianon, but these were merely the prelude to lakeside diplomacy, when the grand hotel would be born.

During the years when the last century was becoming the present one, the old world went through an abrupt change. Railroads shortened distances for the laziest of travellers, and since the idle rich knocking about Europe, or their bankers and the Kings and Princes whose castles had suddenly become too small, required some place to stay, the grand hotel came into being.

Up till now in this book, we have merely described a lavish episode in a minor line of development within the history of civilization. But once these sumptuous and colossal palace hotels of our time had been put up, their owners realized that the establishments need not merely provide dancing, food, drink, and a little, or large, room to sleep in for travellers often seeking other pleasures. Having been erected, moreover, at the heart of cities or in spa towns, the new palaces were surrounded by a whole local population who, of course, had no need to live in them, but who too could use the palatial establishments for eating, drinking, amusing themselves, or even waltzing on parquet floors once trod by Princes and Kings.

Just take a careful look at the great hotels we love so much—the Imperial in Vienna, the Brenner's Park Hotel at Baden-Baden, Budapest's Gellert, or the three great Ritzes, with their monumental foyers, their parade staircases, their dining rooms painted with ecstatic priestesses or seductive goddesses, their labyrinthine corridors, the privacy of the bedrooms and small salons, the mystery of secluded apartments and communicating suites, the hall porters prepared to play so many different roles, not to mention the pretty chambermaids. And then wonder what, after all, theses palaces constructed only yesterday may be if not an exact replica, scaled and styled in relation to a society in full evolution, of the palaces and châteaux of old, their follies included.

Now we can understand that the life led in those new palaces and châteaux—all so splendidly organized for such a purpose, and priced accordingly, even in the tariff was not always discreetly posted on the back of the bathroom door—would be the same as that formerly known in the old châteaux and palaces. Festivity and history would meet again.

Earlier, we spoke of the fabulous dinners, balls, and other amusements the Empress Eugénie arranged for her summer guests at the villa now known by her name, as well as through the art of the Second Empire portraitist Winterhalter. But even in the aftermath of Sédan, the Commune, and the English exile of Napoléon III, the sumptuous residence built in Biarritz by Couvrechef—an architect with a fortuitous name—survived to become the scene of the same, or almost the same, fêtes, balls, and encounters with history. Only the paintings changed. Edward VII, the English King who was more French than anyone dared admit, selected it for his winter season, the better to take care of his weak lungs.

First, however, the Villa Eugénie had become a *propriété nationale* and then the Palais de Biarritz, the luxurious casino inaugurated in 1881 by the Duke of Alba. But following its partial reconstruction in 1905, made necessary by a fire that forced the Grand Duchess Olga, sister of Tsar Nicolas II, to flee half-naked, the Villa Eugénie ceased to be the Palais de Biarritz and became the Hotel du Palais, a virtual branch of the Spanish, Portuguese, and English courts, as famous throughout the world for the feverish pace of its fêtes and galas as for the parade of crowned heads that continued to illuminate its history. From that time forward, the name Hotel du Palais stuck.

With its sculptural busts on the façade and its famous medallions glorifying every woman in the world who is heir to the Empress Eugénie—French, English, Italian, and, of course, Spanish—the Hotel du Palais constitutes something of a symbol. It stands for the chain that links yesteryear to yesterday, for the princely residences where great events and gossip co-mingle, for the turn-of-the-century palaces where hotelier dynasties as renowned as those with thrones built another aristocracy, that of the Ritzes and the Escoffiers who in their own way are the peers of the grandees they have supplanted.

But the Hotel du Palais is not unique. Already we have evoked the Venetian wedding at the Dandolo Palace a mere step or two away from the Bridge of Sighs, with the union of the Giustiniani and Mocenigo families possibly inspiring Strozzi to compose his *Prosperine*. Well, the same Dandolo Palace—which took its name from the Venetian family that entered history when, at the beginning of the thirteenth century, a Dandolo led the Fourth Crusade to Constantinople and thus made Venice a great power—we know today. Albeit rehabilitated and redecorated, like the Villa Eugénie at Biarritz, it became the Danieli, one of the most fabulous hotels in the world, whose glory—the Gothic charm, the marble or copper traceries, the cut glass—survive from the original palace of the Dandoli. Thus, the ancient mansion enjoys as much fame in Venice, or almost, as the Accademia or the Cà d'Oro ; certainly it is more celebrated among tour groups and conventioneers than such secret haunts as the Scuola San Giorgio with its Carpaccios or the San Sebastiano church with its Veroneses. Tourists stop before the narrow door leading to a monumental hall or enter to discover the mysteries of frescoes, stuccoed decorations, and elaborately carved galleries, all making a "lobby" full of chattering people, and they do so with all the respect once reserved for the interiors of the Cà Rezzonico or the few "true" palaces that might be open to them. The Danieli, which began as a palace, has become one again. And 350 years after the festivities of 1629, the Mexican billionaire Charles de Bestegui gave his legendary masked ball on 3 September 1951 at the nearby Palazzo Labbia.

Come from all over the world and costumed by the most famous couturiers in Paris, Bestegui's guests poured into the hotel or into neighbouring palaces. With their diamond-studded dominoes, golden aigrettes, masks decorated by leading painters, and garments shaped by sculptors, anybody to whom the Almanach de Gotha could still attribute a coronet, plus the world of the arts, letters, fashion, and just plain money, waltzed till dawn under cascades of light, the fires from all the jewels filling the atmosphere with a veritable confetti of glittering reflections.

There could be no better cause for celebration than the opening of a new palace, a sumptuous baptism far more spectacular than the births of modern Kings and Princesses. Thus, to return to Venice—and who would not want to go back to that splendid place—the opening of the Excelsior on the Lido, the great rival of the Hotel des Bains, was marked by one of the most fantastic receptions ever seen in the history of grand hotels. Still, the Hotel des Bains, at its own inauguration seven years earlier, in 1901, had drawn an international clientele that filled its galleries, Art Deco salons, and white colonnades to overflowing, till even a few social lions had to be turned away, among the many other aspirants who crowded into that snobbish little kingdom, the Lido.

And so on 21 July 1907 at eleven in the evening, to the sound of music composed expressly for the occasion (the "Excelsior" by which the pigeons of San Marco's sometimes still dance between the Café Florian and the Quadri), thousands of flares and illuminations made the night sky blaze for hours like a great multicoloured art work, created by one of Italy's most celebrated pyrotechnists. Thirty thousand Venetians and tourists had crossed the lagoon in gondolas or simpler craft, all determined to witness a once-in-a-lifetime party thrown in honour of an hotel like none other ever seen. From the Piazza San Marco to the beach they voyaged through canals festooned with garlands and Venetian lanterns, moving towards the hotel's pale façade alive with reflections cast up by the lapping lagoon.

Watched by thirty thousand curiosity-seekers, three thousands guests—the kings and queens of industry or the arts, those uncrowned royals of Venice, Italy, and the whole of Europe, made merry in the salons of the ground and first floors, in the Dutch garden, and on the terrace along the sea. While the guests dined at four separate banquets, all served simultaneously, gypsy orchestras played round the tables. Afterwards, dancing went on till six in the morning, well after dawn. Legend has it—and hotels always have their legends—that no one left the Excelsior on that inaugural occasion before the last violin had played its final note.

Meanwhile, a bit later or a bit earlier, history was taking its course at the rival Hotel des Bains. The blond boy Tadzio, beautiful as an angel and as silent as the cherubim on the Annunziata ceilings above him, played among the columns and on the beach under the gaze of Aschenbach, Thomas Mann's old dying musician on a visit to Venice. It was in 1913 that the author of *Buddenbrooks*, and the yet-to-come *Magic Mountain*, arrived at the Hotel des Bains and made literary history, for it was there, between the sky and the sea, that he suddenly had the idea for *Death in Venice*. Sixty years later, Luchino Visconti set up his cameras and brought the Hotel des Bains, freshly made up for the occasion, into cinematic history.

The Hotel des Bains entered the history of music that wan morning in 1929 when a man, lying in one of the most beautiful rooms of that dawn-quiet palace, had one last glimpse of the sun rising over the horizon above the sea. A lone tear slipped down his cheek. Serge Lifar, who was there, called it a diamond. The man with the single tear was none other than the great Diaghilev, who had restored dance to Europe and now died bathed in the world's grandest light, between the time dawn broke over the sea and the time it took for a jewelled tear to congeal on his face. It was 5 : 45 on an August morning when Diaghilev played his final scene at the Hotel des Bains.

Too sad, this story ? Certainly not. Those palaces that now seem to defy time have become important places in so many lives, and life itself is a destiny played out under the gilded cornices of our dream palaces. Where else did the Empress Elizabeth of Austria, the Sissi of legend and the films she inspired, go to die but in an hotel that resembled the set for an operetta ?

Switzerland has two Beau-Rivages : one in Lausanne, which seems to be right in step with history, and the other in Geneva, an intimate place with its extraordinary balcony, running from floor to floor above an entrance hall that, from above, resembles a huge case of glass, marble, and wood. The same kind of lacework, moulded of bronze cast in Italy and mounted above a void, can be seen at Denver's Brown Palace Hotel, built for the American Gold Rush. There one could have a' rip-snorting time, gamble for big stakes, and cross the street by underground passage to the Navarre, where the ladies waited. Geneva's Beau Rivage offered something quieter, a sumptuous moment suspended in a gilded cage for little exotic birds. But it was under its balconies, where one can imagine Zerbinetta or Despina, little servant girls with white petticoats and light blouses, calling to one another from floor to floor, that they brought Franz-Joseph's wife, like a great wounded swallow, stabbed in the heart by an anarchist with a stiletto so thin that at first the Empress seemed only to have suffered a pin prick. She was on her way to take one of those white boats that cross Lac Léman when suddenly she raised a hand to her breast. "It's nothing...." They carried her to the nearest hotel and, between Mayerling and Sarajevo, the Austro-Hungarian monarchy retreated a bit further into its twilight. The Despinas and Zerbinettas had stopped their laughter on the wooden galleries.

In nearby Lausanne, at the other Beau-Rivage, it was peace that became the issue. History, as we all know, is no longer made in royal palaces. The Italo-Turkish Conference of 1912, the Lausanne Conference of 1922-23, the Reparations Conference of 1933—all took place at Lausanne's Beau-Rivage. Then early in 1984 came the meeting of all parties involved in the Lebanese crisis, complete with bodyguards, whole families, and swarms of journalists. Born with the Simplon-Orient Express, Lausanne's Beau-Rivage, has become one of the essential squares on the extravagant chessboard where, from international meeting to European conference, the game of world peace is played out. Today, indeed, but already yesterday, a diplomacy long past that of the Congress of Vienna has almost become a lakeside diplomacy.

It was in 1933 that the Hotel des Îles Borromées, halfway between the setting of Hemingway's *Farewell to Arms* and the fabulous palpitations of La Duse and d'Annunzio, sheltered the heads of state and the Italian, English, and French ministers during the Stresa Conference. This conference, as well as a thousand other secret meetings, from the Hotel des Iles Borromées to the Villa d'Este on Lake Como, have held Europe spellbound with their illusory peace and their great moments of hope.

From the very beginning, palace hotels have been the scenes of dancing, death, and attempts to save the future. And that is where we still await the coming of better days.

How many monarchs were, only yesterday, spending their exile in the world's palace hotels ? And how many heads of state—of dismembered republics—during the period when the Nazi flag flew high over Europe ? During the last World War, Claridge's in London became a kind of protected residence for all those driven from their own palaces : George II of Greece, who called himself Mr. Brown ; Raczkiewiscz, the embodiment of Polish vigilance and hope ; Queen Wilhelmina of The Netherlands ; King Haakon of Norway ; not to mention Jugoslavia's Peter II and Greece's Princess Alexandra, who, early in 1944, married, with neither fanfare nor carriage but merely conveyed to church in the private limousine of George VI, whose guests, after all, they were, even in the grand hotel.

It is true that Claridge's, with its immense stairway, which seems to soar in voluptuous convolutions above the great hall, with its miles of polished copper, its flowers and vases like none other in hotels anywhere, its ballroom chandeliers imported directly from the Paris World's Fair of 1900, offers everything that could be expected of a royal residence at a time when none can ever again be constructed. Thus, there is the inevitable legend—this time corroborated by every apartment, every little room, the most luxurious of all the suites—which, since it is, after all, Claridge's, becomes a private matter that must be discussed with the director privately. At Claridge's, for example, they know how to keep track of what remains in the thinning wallet of a dethroned sovereign, as well as in the bulging billfold of another—modern and oil-rich—King.

Every great hotel has a unique style, compounded of its clientele and the sort of day and night life that takes place there. While Claridge's may seem a bastion of aristocracy, a living Almanach de Gotha, the Savoy on the Thames Embankment resembles an open club of artists, theatre folk, writers, clowns, and other entertainers. But the Savoy too has its dramas and celebrations. The hotel is quite literally a child of the theatre, since it began, splendour and all, with the theatre built for the D'Oyly Carte Company, which existed to perform the operas of Gilbert and Sullivan. Thus, the Savoy invented the operetta-like party, such as the glorious one staged in the manner of *The Gondoliers*, which entailed flooding the hotel's interior courtyard. For the illusion to be complete, it required only that boats on the Thames be decorated as Venetian gondolas, thus taking us back to the old Dandolo or the new Danieli. More garlands and lanterns, like those at the Lido's Excelsior, more fireworks and thousand-carat jewels. The prince of this folly was none other than Enrico Caruso, who even arrived by gondola, lit by four hundred chandeliers, and sang for the hundreds of guests invited by billionaire George Kessler. Mad about "stomping at the Savoy", Kessler arranged another banquet, this time at Christmas, and, for the occasion, had the hotel's floors covered with fake snow and the walls of every salon and dining room decorated with snow-white chrysanthemums. Since Kessler never did anything by halves, he gave each of his guests cigarette cases made by Cartier.

*Menu-dated January 1st. 1892 - of the* Hôtel Quirinale, *Rome.*

While at Claridge's the Queen is honoured once a year for her involvement in England's great turf events, at the Savoy the chefs invent dishes in honour of divas and lovers of the good life that have beguiled palates all over the world. The *Cuisses de Nymphes à l'Aurore* made for the Prince of Wales—the future Edward VIII—consist of frogs' legs served in a *gelée* made of cream and wine seasoned with paprika. As for Pêche Melba, its origins are obscure, other than the fact that the dessert may have been made by the famous Escoffier, that chef of chefs, who concocted it for the great Nellie Melba, the Australian soprano who could sing Lucia, Violetta, and Brünhilde, all in rotation. But it was also for her, at a time when the not-so-fragile Valkyrie wanted merely to nibble at something light, that Escoffier thought up Melba Toast, and for her too that he created *Poularde Tosca*, which, were all things logical, should have been called *Poularde au Sang*. Then there was that other illustrious song bird, Luisa Tetrazzini, another Lucia and Violetta—for whom the chef, still at the Savoy and no doubt eager not to exacerbate the operatic rivalries, invented *Poularde Belle Hélène*, perhaps better known in the English-speaking world as Chicken Tetrazzini. Here, history, music, and fine cuisine mix with the voices of women who knew how to touch the heart.

When it comes to history and drama, the Savoy has had them in its own legendary way. Take, for instance, the time of the Blitz in London, when all the while that bombs were raining down on the British capital, Carol Gibbons' orchestra continued to play for a ballroom full of dancers in evening attire. Suddenly, a bomb fell in the Strand outside and the blast from the explosion swept the platform clean of its musicians. First, there was silence, and then a man picked himself up. He went to the piano and, hardly missing a beat, began to play and sing! Little by little, calm returned, and as people listened, they broke into song after song. While the bombs continued falling on London, the old city had one of the best evenings of its war years. True enough, the smiling and amused singer happened to be Noël Coward.

Once a grand hotel enters history, the thousand and one anecdotes and bits of legend are retailed by generation after generation of porters and maîtres d'hôtel, always in a tone of veneration. This is why the Hotel de Paris in Monte Carlo—all volutes and glazed terraces facing the Casino and the no less sublime "little" Garnier Opéra, besieged by a never-ending procession of limousines and celebrity-hounds—retains its own archivist charged with keeping scrupulous account of who of any note or anecdotal worth ever stayed there.

It is the archivist who reports that the Grand Duke Michael of Russia, to make certain that he reach the Monegasque capital and his apartment in the hotel, insisted that his special train—here the legend of grand hotels coalesces with that of luxury trains—not exceed fifty kilometres per hour. Never mind that it created serious congestion on the rails and delays all along the line. Once there, Grand Dukes Michael and Dimitri took whole floors in the hotel, and then emptied sixty magnums of champagne one night just to wash down some hundreds of blinis with caviar, all the while surrounded by pretty women and the very best freeloaders. Given their story value, should we pardon such fabulous high livers?

Then there is the tale of Toby the parakeet, Churchill's faithful pet, which could not resist the blue Mediterranean sky, the palms, and the casino's Second Empire façades and flew away. The desperate Churchill called up every reserve, including the fire brigade's tallest ladder. The parakeet could be seen gliding through the air, from tree to tree, till the British statesman, watching from his balcony, lost sight of the bird as night fell. For Churchill it was a grave matter, and so he offered a reward of 150 francs for the return of his beloved Toby. The next morning the great hall was filled with more than a hundred persons, all queued up and each carrying a cage with a parakeet inside. Alas, none of them was Toby, but Churchill took consolation—little does it matter whether the occasion was this one or another—in a bottle of old brandy, whose cork—pulled just in time—bore the date 1810. A Napoleonic brandy 150 years later. It is of just such moments that, finally, *ententes cordiales* are made!

The history of great events and gossip rolls on, from palace to palace. And from palace to palace we find the same figures—Churchill, the Aga Khan, or Josephine Baker. It was at the Bristol—Paris's sumptuous Bristol, so recently restored—that the great black lady died, following a spectacular fête, attended by Grace of Monaco, Alain Delon, Jeanne Moreau, and Jean-Claude Brialy. La Baker had worn a sensational white gown. Several days later they buried her in the same dress, and the friends who gathered about her for the last time were the very ones who had been at the great party. The Josephine Baker they bade farewell looked younger and more beautiful than ever.

Today, is it possible to say that these fabulous soirées, these eccentricities of the world's great, and the palaces' rendez-vous with history truly belong to History? Perhaps the era of wild parties has somewhat passed; at least, the Ritz and Claridge's seem to have fewer of them, those Arabian Night receptions that social historians remember with such emotion. To begin with, there are, other than some new but genuine Arabian Night Princes, fewer and fewer sybaritic guests who can afford to transform the Savoy into a Venetian lagoon. Still, the contemporary age brings its own myths to the rescue.

For instance, there is the world of ski or the film world. Today, everyone, or almost everyone, skis, but the most splendid skiers are those who rarely go near the slopes. May the habitués and sportsmen of St-Moritz forgive me, but the entire world knows that it is not for the skiing that one checks in at the St-Moritz Palace. Rather, it is to see, to be seen, and to take part in some of the last fêtes of our era. Long gone is the time when Baron Maurice de Rothschild, the father of Baron Edouard, regularly ended each of his toboggan parties—he never, of course, set foot on skis—by pulling off his snow-covered trousers right in the middle of the hotel's great hall, to the delight of Princesses and other semi-crowned heads who, in order to be seen, looked on with no little interest.

It was not quite so long ago that Belgium's Baron Empain took over the whole hotel and filled it with mimosa flown in specially from the Côte d'Azur, the occasion being, true enough, to celebrate the mating of St-Moritz with Bormes-les-Mimosas—without himself there to attend his own ball, thanks to a snowstorm that cancelled his flight. But even out in the cold, Empain was among good company, since the shipping magnate Niarchos and the King of Morocco's brother had been detained for the same reason. One makes do with what is at hand, and on this occasion those left to entertain themselves were none other than the Shah of Persia, the president

of Fiat, the wife of Karajan, and a good half-dozen Bourbon-Parmes, Orsinis, Fords, Lichtensteins, and assorted Jugoslavian Princesses, proving that in the seventies the ingredients for a splendid party still existed. But does skiing really have anything to do with it ?

And what about the cinema ? If there is a palace in the world where, since the last World War, the word *fête* still means *folies*, beauty, extravagance, "business", feverish activity, and flash bulbs, it is the Carlton in Cannes. Throughout the year the Carlton, with its terrace on the Croisette, its panelled dining room, its sumptuous apartments, is a slightly solemn, balconied place overlooking the sea, rather like all the other grand hotels. But for three weeks in the spring the palace annually transforms itself into a permanent caravanserai for world films. The Cannes Film Festival, founded on the eve of the Second World War, only to be displaced by Mussolini's Venice festival and then interrupted by the outbreak of hostilities, did not get truly under way until 1947. But immediately, even more than the Casino, the old or the new festival palace—not to mention the *nouveau* Nouveau Palais with its deserts of concrete—the Carlton became the very heart of all the festivities organized for, round, or on the fringes of films. The jury stops at the Carlton, and there is where the stars make their entrances, and where one goes on foot, through crowds of fans two to six deep, to the projection rooms, and it is at the Carlton that everyone returns for supper, the day's duty accomplished, all the while bombarded by photographers who, lurking in the halls, lay siege to anyone who even remotely looks like a film actor.

Whole books have been written on the Cannes Film Festival and on the Carlton. Simply remembering at random, one thinks of that famous photo taken for *Paris Match*, in its prime, showing thirty or forty stars and the like standing all together at a palace window, ranging from Jean Cocteau to Daniel Gélin and representing everything from Rome's Cinecittà to Hollywood. Only a Carlton could have brought off that tour de force of diplomacy and protocol.

From breakfast on the balconies to the last drink at four in the morning in the Carlton's "little bar"—that rococo jewel which for the initiated remains open after every other bar in Cannes, including the hotel's own "large bar", has closed—a day at the Carlton during the Film Festival is a fantastic plunge into the very innards of the Seventh Art. One ogles the stars on the terrace, their presence signalled by the movement of the crowd, whose flow brings them in and then bears them away, watched always by the impassive gaze of waiters and captains as the navigation continues along its tumultuous course. Almost as interesting is the sight of the non-stars playing stars, with their sunglasses and low-cut blouses, desperate to give the impression for one day that they reign like the others.

*Exhibition in the concert hall in the* Hotel Kurhaus, *Scheveningen in 1925.*

There is no end of stories about third-rate producers who tip the bellmen to page them ten times a day in the hope of having it believed they are being called to Hollywood for some miraculous project. Similarly motivated were those tiny starlettes of the fifties who hoped to assure their glory by making an outrageous spectacle of their anatomy on the Carlton's beach. Although the photographers always arrived on time, fame rarely caught up. Meanwhile, one could visually devour Martine Carol, Michèle Morgan, or Gina Lollobrigida, who strode the several metres of magic carpet that ran from the hotel's entrance to the lifts. *La fête* had begun, and it was everywhere.

With the passing years, the Film Festival has become "commercialized". More and more people go to Cannes to make deals rather than to be seen. But anyone who wants to be seen goes to the Carlton to do it—under billboards ten times life-size promoting James Bond as 007 or the heroes of *Star Wars*.

Meanwhile, little by little and by the insistence of backers eager for business to flourish round the calendar, the parties in the palace, with their fireworks and vast expenditures, have become everyday affairs. The directors of these great sumptuous houses, where one can still check in with family and children for a good part of the season, have realized that it takes something more than luxury and a thousand considerations with which they envelop their clients in order to retain them, if not attract new ones. Thus, at the risk of imitating the vacation colonies for overgrown and somewhat retarded children—the clubs offering budget holidays on some sort of substitute Mediterranean at the other end of the world—they have reinvented the art and manner of entertaining the most difficult of guests, those who have already done everything. Of course, there was always the orchestra at tea time, or the band under the canopy in the garden, but now something more is required. Thus, we have the Brenner's Park in Baden-Baden.

To the lush, dreamy paths along the Oos River separating the hotel's private gardens from the Lichtenhaller Allee, a route crossed at the *fin de siècle* by virtually everyone who then counted, something new has been added. In the high season, for instance, chamber orchestras appear in the salons and play Mozart or Haydn. No longer must one be the guest of a Prince or a rich arms merchant to taste such rarefied pleasures as a string quartet playing, apparently, just for you. Brenner's welcomes you both before and after dinner. You can even participate in bridge, tennis, or backgammon tournaments organized by the hotel's management. Moreover, there are galas for singles taking the cure, and anyone dressed in a dinner jacket or a long dress can waltz in the ivory-colonnaded salon, the three-quarter time also provided just for you, and thus partake of a kind of luxury once thought gone forever but now revived. It is like an orgy of nostalgia fed by Strauss and Lehar.

Then there is the notice in at least three languages on the vestibule of every apartment: "Gentlemen, ladies appreciate your dressing for the evening...". Although only suggested and not de rigueur, the black bow-tie on a starched white shirt is strongly urged.

When August arrives, bringing with it the big week of horse racing, palace life seems utterly unchanged, a world where an air of festivity prevails round the clock. Apartments must, almost always, be reserved from one year to the next, and now everyone wears the proper evening attire. Even the buffet lunches are more opulent than ever, and the teas served in late afternoon are of a sort one had forgotten ever existed. Moreover, diamonds come out in force at the end of a day spent in the paddock, but at Brenner's Park in Baden-Baden the racing week is merely the logical conclusion to a season that will re-commence as soon as the last horse has arrived at the stables.

What has been understood in this palace, born out of mineral-water baths and made into a self-contained city, its rococo or neoclassical façades facing eternally green gardens, its covered swimming pool resembling a Roman bath open to manicured lawns, its porters displaying a courtesy exceeding anything we have encountered in all our hotel experience, is that *la fête* must be a daily event, in the arcade lined with luxury shops, among the fountains whose rise and fall follow the rhythm of an orchestra playing in a kiosk. The pleasure is that of another age, precious, obviously expensive, and heart-warming.

Now at the end of this brief escape into often magical realms, I suddenly regret having not mentioned other equally miraculous palaces. The Crillon, for instance, the world's most beautiful grand hotel, with its enormous cocktails served in the first-floor salons, their tall window-doors open to the Place de la Concorde. I also think of Gleneagles, in the heart of Scotland, where golf is king, a city built all of a piece, a gigantic stone ship beached by the storms that break over the heaths, where one makes obeisance, in bermudas at noon but in evening clothes at night, to the joy of eighteen holes and the *après-golf*—and savours the most sumptuous of Sunday buffets. Finally, there is the Goldener Hirsch in Salzburg, the most delicate and refined, the most delightfully snobbish of the world's grand hotels, where they gravely reply on 1 January that you are on the waiting list for dinner round the 1st of August. Since Mozart reigns in Salzburg, only Karajan has carte blanche, and to take supper at the Goldener Hirsch following a performance of *Rosenkavalier* or *Don Giovanni* entails diplomacy of a high order but also the most exquisite of pleasures.

And so, empires may crumble, the dollar rise or fall, the great of this world made smaller and smaller, but the luxurious life of grand hotels survives forever. Whether it is a ball of bewildering beauty or the sober intimacy of a supper after the opera, from palace to palace *la fête* lives on, and History is often a rendez-vous. It is up to you to make it so.

*Edward VII at the* Hôtel du Palais, *Biarritz.*

# THROUGH THE LOOKING GLASS

## FRÉDÉRIC GRENDEL

Within these marvellous structures, where time seems to have stopped, even as the clock ticks away, each of us is Alice.

More than anything else, a palace is a looking glass, its silvery surface, polished by unseen hands, reflecting an old and luxurious dream, a dream populated by Kings and actresses, sometimes by minor lords and bit players.

Alice longs to see the other side, the forbidden realm. But between the right and wrong sides of the décor is a threshold which, while fragile, seems to be uncrossable by travellers. Meanwhile, these clients cannot be unaware of the young, fleet-footed troupe that pour in from the wings, or disappear, suddenly like lizards.

Undoubtedly a two-sided, or reversible, longing places society, whose common denominator is a room key, face to face with the tireless army whose password takes the form of a pass key.

Clad in black and white, a scheme becoming to creatures who dip in and out of the dark, the servants, both male and female, proffer without knowing it, or knowing it just slightly, their fugitive grace, which seems all the greater for being inaccessible.

Bedecked or dressed in basic black, the hard-pressed and the powerful tender one another their respective wealth, whether visible or virtual.

Rarely upset by either side, this equilibrium or high tension between two incommunicable worlds — this mute and almost always punished longing — divides the palaces like a knife sliced into a fruit.

To know the hidden face of the grand European hotels, the would-be visitor should proceed by successive incursions. A palace cannot be turned inside out like a glove. Beyond the looking glass, the gilt, and the marble lie the necessary suburbs of the world of dreams.

Once a tapestry has been woven, its reverse side looks like nothing. Examining those ends of multicoloured wool, all knotted and frayed, who could imagine a unicorn or the strange martyrdom of Saint Sebastian ? There would appear to be no correspondence between the two faces of the fabric. Yet, even the tiniest thread is essential to a figure, and that bit of yellow, pulled through the canvas centuries ago, constitutes the root of a buttercup.

In the chill labyrinth, Alice or Ariadne, provided she does not lose her way, should follow the pipes running side by side above her head. For more than a century in all the palaces of the world — in London, Paris, Venice, Istanbul, New York — the same pipes make corridors, iron stairways, impasses, pits, and flies all resemble the gangplanks of ocean liners. Such

*Three generations of hoteliers and future hoteliers: the Armleder family, founders of the* Hôtel Richemond, *Geneva.*
*Left page:*
*The* Hôtel Prince de Galles, *Paris.*

fantastic tubing, its purpose often unknown, must be concealed at all cost in order not to offend the eyes of passengers, whether they go in pursuit of a chimera or a project. If the palace is not enchanted, the voyager will change either his category or his destination. Once in his suite, or in Room 104, the foreigner forgets all scientific facts. For him, or for his pleasure, water flows from the wall, heat or cool rises in his apartment. He is in a closed environment, magical and cut free of all moorings to reality.

Everything not meant to be seen, or even suspected is systematically consigned to the domestic penumbra. Unlike the hotels built today, where function implacably becomes form, the great palaces provide the last resort of the irrational and the fanciful.

But to last, without intermission, the madness must be maintained, scheduled, supervised, and programmed. The queen bee, within her royal cell, does not know, and has no reason to know, anything about the methodical hosts labouring in the background in order that she may sip her jelly.

Naturally, in the grand hotels royalty is shared. Depending on the establishment's capacity, and the frequency of the visits, Kings and Queens may be as many as a hundred, often a great deal more numerous. Man being, it is said, higher than the bees, the workers in hotel service are proportionately less numerous than those in a beehive.

Surrounding a number or a key — that is, the room and its contents — the number of supporting personnel has varied since the nineteenth century, and in recent years it has markedly declined. Formerly, there might have been as many as a thousand souls serving a hundred room numbers. Today, in certain old palaces, especially in Great Britain, the ratio still remains four to one.

But the modernization of equipment, more rational management, and the abandonment of some outmoded livery now make it possible for there to be a more exact balance between masters and servants. In the Hôtel de Crillon, smarted up, restored, but more sumptuous than ever, the entire one-hundred-member staff does not exceed an equal number of guests.

However, nothing prevents our recalling, somewhat nostalgically, the grand hotel operas of yesteryear when, once through the revolving door, Monsieur Perrichon immediately became the Prince of Wales, or at least Perrichon's idea of what that might mean.

Preparing to write the dialogue for a film back in the fifties, I had reserved a room for a sojourn of several days at the Hôtel Normandy. It was the end of winter, or at least the middle of February, when Deauville had all gears in neutral and was simply idling.

When I, a very ordinary guest, arrived, having walked the five or six metres from the station, I found myself received with a respect totally unrelated to my status in life. After much bowing and scraping, and several rather singular ceremonies, the head receptionist invited me to follow him into the lift, the leather walls of which reeked of wax. On the first floor we caught up with the porter and two or three footmen, dispatched no doubt to clear the way for us. But I had seen nothing yet. In the wide corridor, near the room where I was to live with my characters, stood at least a dozen worker bees, all lined up in perfect formation, if not in perfectly matched uniforms, with their wings laid back but their antennae quivering.

We lost no time in getting to know one another. Thanks to information distilled from a duotone voice — an Oxonian accent occasionally imposing itself on southern sounds — by the man in a jacket, I soon knew who would bring a bottle of champagne and who might make the cork pop ; I got to know the face of the fellow who, at three in the morning, would scramble my eggs in the bain-marie, and who would serve them to me ; I was presented with the hall clerk, the valet, the two chambermaids, the linen maid, the seamstress, and a fourth footman who I already imagined would be running to the Rue des Italiens to fetch me a copy of *Le Monde* before dinner ; and, finally, I discovered the one person without whom nothing else could be on the floor : the head housekeeper. As the troupe passed in review, the chief receptionist gave assurances that the whole of this little world would, on a sign from me, jump right out the window, and I believed it. These were good times, and they even seemed to be for good.

Before the great wars, the principal function of the floor personnel was to wait in the pantry or in little alcoves in front of the bell board. In theory, a servant could spend a whole day — conceivably an entire season — without leaving his chair or stool. If no one was thirsty, the sommelier simply had to bottle up in solitary boredom.

Behind the scenes, the division of labour is carried to the point of eccentricity. A hall porter, whose sole function is to transport and deliver breakfasts, or other meals taken in the room, whatever the hour of day or night, could never, without losing status, pick up a feather duster. If perchance he should feel inspired to pluck so much as a hair from the arm of a chair, the incident might very well end with his getting sacked.

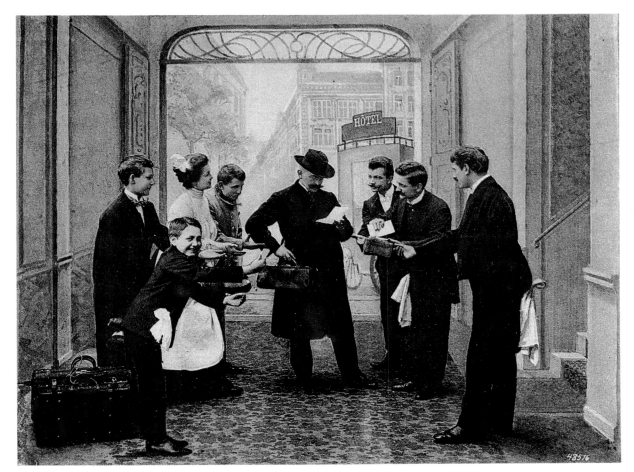

*Tipping:*
*an early nineteenth*
*century postcard.*

We are in the theatre, and very close to the stage on which several comedies are being played at once. Each member of the cast must stay within the limits of his assigned role ; Tartufe cannot without considerable risk begin speaking the lines of Orgon. By the same token, the valet de chambre may not dream, even for a second, of tightening a leaky tap.

This discipline and the extreme specialization of tasks, which, as we shall see, sometimes goes hand in hand with a quasi-military respect for hierarchy, may actually protect an employee who, behind his or her uniform, is sound asleep.

The apartment or the room may on occasion become a danger zone for the service personnel. By moving through the door, in response to some ever-imperious summons, the hall porter, the footman, or the linen maid runs a double risk, since each of them passes directly from a public area to a closed, intimate space, where even the air is different, having been charged throughout the night with odours and sometimes with electricity. Then, for an instant, roles are reversed. The domestic becomes the client of his own curiosity and, intentionally or not, a furtive voyeur. One cannot imagine the diversity, and often the indecency, of the morning spectacle. But, as already noted, the celebrity or importance of those present, and without any reason to conceal their presence, simply adds to the peril, sometimes even doubling it. The diva's half-seen knee weighs more heavily on a subordinate's libido than the full view of what the French call *l'académie bourgeoise*, a euphemism for the nude body. Now is when a very formal comportment, rigorously maintained, serves as a break or, if you will, a step on the gas. In life on the hotel floor, the habit makes the monk.

Certain kinds of hotel workers venture onto the stage only rarely. These are the repairmen. Usually, they can be seen up in the flies — that is, just under the roof, in the little servants' quarters, formerly reserved for domestics travelling with their employers. Today hotel guests have changed their entourage, with the bodyguard and the private secretary replacing the zealous shadows of old, and, unlike the latter, occupying rooms near the apartment taken by their lord and master. Up in the now-liberated mansard labour all sorts of artisan : furniture makers, carpenters, polishers, weavers, and, even more, painters, plumbers, and electricians. For several years a specialist in air conditioning has taken his place down in the basement along with the team of boilermen. But as always, such people operate under a leader, in this instance the engineer responsible for maintenance services.

There remains one category of worker whose faces no hotel guest ever sees : the launderers. It would be difficult to conceive of the number of sheets, pillow cases of various sorts, bathrobes and towels, washcloths, tablecloths, and tray linen that an hotel must launder and iron every day. In the grand hotels, where rooms count in the hundreds, the head of the laundry service becomes an essential cog in the organizational wheel. The men and women subject to his orders come and go in an atmosphere somewhat like that of a Turkish bath. While ignoring what may be going on to the left or the right, each person goes about his task. Heating the water, mopping up, sorting, pressing, folding, mangling — the whole business of making the linen sparkle — are all distinct and different operations. The manglers, with their turning cylinders and rollers, disdain the ironers, and vice versa. In that humid netherworld, there is, as everywhere else, the beautiful linen and that which is less so.

Far from being hidden away, the florists and gardeners live in the out-of-doors, ableit closely tied to the main building, somewhat like the cosmonauts who leave their metal capsule to take a walk in space. The Ritz Hotels have their own greenhouses, and some hotels carry luxury to the point of replanting their terraces and urns overnight. Thus, a garden that is red on Tuesday may have become white by dawn on Wednesday.

Swimming instructors, bathhouse attendants, and masseurs appear and disappear with the beginning and end of the season, for when the pool is empty, the saunas are full.

Water and steam emanate from yet another corner of the establishment. But closed in like a world apart and governed by mysterious laws, the kitchens serve totally different purposes. They are parts of the whole but have nothing in common with the rest. In the world of the grand hotel, they are to a certain degree foreigners. Entering the kitchen is tantamount to crossing a frontier. Beyond the wall of tile, brick, or glass, the air itself seems hardly recognizable. Whoever steps over the line, with whatever special permit, becomes immediately prey to his senses. Like an addict, he discovers unknown sounds, distinguishes noises even to the smallest rubbing, and moves straightaway from the singular to the plural. But even more, it is the odours that produce the rarest sensations. Soon, he will be able to get high all by himself simply by inhaling the whole atmosphere and then separating from the composite smell the unique, exact fragrance of a truffle being diligently brushed by an assistant.

Only yesterday the kitchen depended on coal, which, despite the suffocating heat that kept both the chef and the walls permanently streaked with sweat, left one's back shiveringly cold. Built for the most part about a century ago, blackened immediately thereafter, layered in grease, malodorous, always filled with smoke, filthy, cluttered and disorderly, generally located in the basement, the kitchens were a menace to health, safety, and cuisine alike. Still, day after day, chefs of every age, working elbow to elbow, in a promiscuity that sometimes ended in rows, drew from their dark, squalid cavern veritable splendours of gourmandise, dishes composed like Baroque châteaux, and courses of manic complexity, as well as soufflés with the lightness of balloons, Holy Alliance pheasants, and, what else but, Sacred Hearts in spun sugar or nougatine, wimpled like nuns with coffee, and soaked in alcohol to become babas.

These miraculous caverns have all but disappeared, and the futuristic laboratories of today would drive a rat into neurasthenia, and any stray cockroach to madness.

Since the dark days, the kitchen has without doubt become the brightest and best-ventilated part of the entire building. The layout of its equipment, while extremely costly, has been the subject of quasi-scientific research, with the utilization of space cleverly calculated. Once the various stations were fixed, and each piece of equipment installed, the direction of the flow, taking into account all the possibilities — that is, unforeseeable incidents — could be established, and nothing will ever change the order of things, nor infract its rules.

Imagine the surprise of those old chefs if they could see today's sophisticated ovens, whose interior temperature can be raised a hundred degrees in three minutes (microwaves) and whose usable heat is evenly spread, or could try the new pressure cookers, which, unlike boiling water, leave vegetables with their flavour intact.

Fundamentally, however, nothing has changed. The staff remains as numerous as ever, all interrelated in the same immutable hierarchy. And when it comes to knowledge, to the great recipes, secrets, tricks of the trade, they continue to be the same. Of course, cuisine has evolved in the sense that it now tends towards lightness, with less fat and less cooking, all consistent with shifts in the market. But this change, which, if not in keeping with the *taste* of customers, at least corresponds to their rather morbid concern over cholesterol, delights chefs whose art has nothing to do with gluttony, whether *petit bourgeois* or princely.

To be sure, women are barred from these precincts. Apart from a certain class of hotel, cuisine constitutes an exclusively masculine domain. Why ? Because, I'm tempted to respond, that's

*Right page, top:
the kitchens in the* Hôtel
Astoria, *Brussels;
bottom: page boy at
the* Savoy *retrieving game.*

the way it is ! Here and there, women have full responsibility for great restaurants, and, without the slightest drama, they direct teams made up of both sexes. Perfectly honourable hotels in Italy, Spain, and France owe their gastronomic reputations essentially to the women in charge of their kitchens.

Still, the kitchens of the grand European hotels hold firm as the last refuge of virile pretensions, now that the army accepts skirts, and actually solicits them in time of need. Young women have even penetrated the men's locker room at sporting events, all the way to the showers, where blasé athletes no longer notice them. In the hotel kitchen, however, it is men everywhere, as many as forty or fifty, sometimes more. Inevitably, about two out of three wear the immaculate white toque, which makes even the smallest dwarf seem like a giant. Governed by directorial ritual and the undisputed authority of the chef, the hotel kitchen fairly bustles, all in the proper order, with one or more principal sous-chefs, a sous-chef for sauces, another for side dishes, for the pantry, for fish, then on to the sous-chef in charge of grilling and his opposite number at the roasting oven and spit, the sous-chef for hors-d'œuvre, the *potager*, the *friturier, pâtissier,* and *glacier,* a floating sous-chef, sometimes a baker and even a butcher, each an officer in his own right in command of his own brigade of permanent or floating assistants, the whole staff, finally, supported by a suite of *garçons de cuisine.* A woman, however asexual she might be, would not survive a single day in such a college.

Add to this uppercrust such small fry as the whole array of dish washers specializing in pots, glassware, silver, etc., each with a title (*plongeurs de batterie, vaisseliers, verriers, argentiers*), a somewhat colonial population onto which the white, betoqued aristocracy load all kinds of drudgery.

More than a half-century ago, long before he had written *1984,* George Orwell laboured in the scullery at Paris's Hotel Lotti, where he bore the yokes laid on him by the chefs. He may very well have scrubbed a plate soiled by Igor Stravinski, who had already become an habitué of that Parisian palace, but on the right side of the décor.

Near the kitchen, or as little distant as possible, are the dining rooms, the two worlds separated by pantries, vestibules, turntables, and, in the worst of arrangements, redoubtable stairways and dumbwaiters. The journey made by the dining-room staff often doubles or even triples in high season, when guests expect to take their meals in interior courts, among the orange trees, and on the terraces.

The table settings conform to eternal rules, and for the hotel's owner or manager, they bring the moment of truth. There is no way to cut corners when it comes to the quality of linen, the condition and beauty of tablecloths, the perfect match of the china, silver, and crystal, the originality of the accessories and the shape of the bouquets. While some dining rooms may be the very nadir of charm and others about as gay as a morgue, I have seen a number that were enchanting, and the arrival of diners did nothing to disenchant them. Everything depends on a look or a touch, or perhaps the spirit of the director, meaning the head maître d'hôtel.

As for the couvert or place setting, mention must be made, alas, of a revolution the date of whose genesis I cannot cite, but whose deplorable effects I see almost every day. The table silver has, surreptitiously, been turned over ! This event — and it is one — is of concern only to France, and two or three neighbouring regions. For the last thirty or fifty years, possibly longer, France, which throughout centuries had been indisputably above challenge in matters of etiquette and usage, has renounced its primacy. Formerly in this country, spoons and forks rested with their tips and tines turned down, towards the table surface, whereas in the rest of Europe and the world, they were placed the other way round, with their ends turned up like a baby's legs. The difference was dictated by the placement of the cipher, the mark or monogram, a brief form of interlaces engraved in gold, vermeil, or silver. Tradition and French rationality required that the device appear on the right side of the table service. Elsewhere in Europe, possibly to maintain some distance from Paris, spoons and forks were engraved on the reverse side. Then, no doubt in the aftermath of the 1914-1918 war, French restaurateurs began to give way, taking with them hoteliers, ministers, and society. The grand hotels held on for a while, but today they have all, shamelessly, turned their silver. Indeed, only the navy has resisted, whether on the high seas or in port.

This unique shift in usage, regrettable as it may be, has in no way altered the order, the hierarchy, or the implacable organization of the personnel responsible for the dining room. The head maître d'hôtel is incontestably the generalissimo in command of a battlefield. And I use the military terminology quite deliberately, for the adjutants of the head waiter are called *maîtres d'hôtels de carré,* as if they were deputy commanders ! Thus, it is by design that I have ignored the restaurant manager, who is somewhat like a minister, a civilian dependent upon officers

and soldiers. He visits, reviews the troops, salutes a great deal, and, finally, has a permanent smile on his face.

The carver, albeit under the maître d'hôtel, has the advantage of performing a special service, like the sommelier, whose independent spirit is well known. Carving and cutting involve qualities and skills that not everyone can acquire. Then come the line captains with their assistants or waiters (*commis de rang, commis de suite*), the busboys, etc.

Here more than anywhere else, everyone is subject to the rule of his immediate superior in the hierarchy, and sometimes to his excesses. In the dining room, intellectual authority, experience, age, physical power, and even racial instincts yield to hierarchical reality. During and after the dining hour, Einstein would bow before the most monumental fool if he happened to be his chief. Never would a black see his rank challenged by whites wherever these are his assistants. And responsible unions, which sometimes remove a general director, would not venture

Hôtel Ritz, *Paris:*
*the restaurant manager,*
*M. Olivier*
*and a chambermaid.*
*Left page :*
*the* Grand Hôtel
*de Bagnoles-de-l'Orne.*

to defend a busboy, however much he may have been the object of repeated cruelties, if it meant implicating his tormentor as long as the latter is also the busboy's maître.

In the grand hotels — at least in those which have not yet sacrificed their reputations for the sake of profitability — two or three persons should be considered as belonging to a class apart, most especially the head barman. But I should immediately correct this remark by adding that the sovereignty of the barman, his sacred character, and that je-ne-sais-quoi which placed him above the entire system become less distinct with the passing years.

In the old days, guests stayed in their palaces a whole month, sometimes longer. Every year the traveller returned to his apartment, his chambermaids, his table, his waiter, and his barman.

Between the respectable guest and the barman — providing the latter possessed three required qualities : a certain mental finesse, a sense of humour, and native good will — there often developed a privileged relationship, in any event something finer than what went on quite naturally between the guest and the concierge, who may have been an ordinary guardian angel or a commonplace demon, but never a friend. With the bartender, the man on his stool who has had a bit too much, a fifth dry martini, for example, bares his soul more readily and sometimes says in one line more than he ever would to his psychiatrist. And this reciprocal friendship often goes together with a kind of financial trust. Today, at a time when guests are people in a hurry, who rarely spend more than forty-eight hours in the same place, close relations across the bar seem less frequent. Even so, I know an elderly lady, a bit of a millionaire and a bit bankrupt, who occasionally takes an aeroplane just to put the touch on A, a Parisian barman of her own age, who has never asked for the shadow of a receipt, and who, I know for a fact, does not even have her address in Rome.

The concierge, about whom so much has been written, would of course have noted the address of Princess L, in admitting that he had agreed to help her out of a tight spot. As I have suggested, it takes considerable good will, and an ounce of humour, to allow that some guest has run out of cheques, has lost his credit cards, or would rather be chopped up alive than call his banker.

On the other hand, the concierge unflinchingly carries out most of the tasks assigned to him, even though the performance of his duties is conditioned by the wishes of his clientele. Nowadays increasingly fugitive and less original, the members of that clientele all manifest the same quirks and make the same demands. The conciergerie becomes ever-more specifically a travel and theatre-ticket agency. But within this realm the service may work wonders.

Even now, however, Europe can boast here and there concierges whose power extends beyond the opera box office or airline reservations and actually becomes a kind of political force. This develops on those occasions when the concierge must free a guest detained by the police for having knocked down three pedestrians with his Jaguar, or persuade the medical authorities to forget certain requirements in order to protect the private life of one or more individuals — that is, find in time, meaning a matter of hours, the false papers necessary to permit the immediate departure of a guest in danger.

These interventions — exceedingly rare, needless to say, and limited to certain unstable countries — undoubtedly make for colourful anecdotes, but they bear no relationship to modern reality. Moreover, it would be highly improper to see the concierge as a middleman in command of every resource, every sex, every frontier. Addresses, of course, a telephone number perhaps, but as for the rest, the present-day, run-of-the-mill concierge, with rare exceptions, does nothing more than furnish itineraries.

At the same time, however, the concierge has a long reach within the hotel itself, and that is where he can exercise his numerous gifts. Already in charge of the porters, grooms, and pages, he may occasionally extend his empire all the way to the attic. Indeed, like the bartender in certain circumstances, the concierge is subject to no authority, except possibly that of the general director. But this does not mean that a conflict between these two powers must automatically turn to the advantage of the latter. In the 1960s, the concierge at the Plaza-Athénée in Paris, after a brief show of force, won out over the management, whose place he took in the most orderly way possible. Absolute master of his ship, the first to allow the staff a share in the profits of the enterprise, after having increased these to a considerable degree, the former concierge climbed to the very top of the ladder and finally assumed the presidency of a whole chain of hotels. This ascent, while enough to fire the imaginations of every groom, page, or lowly busboy, constitutes little more than an exception that proves the rule.

Relations between the concierge and the reception staff are execrable. However, they seem to improve where a certain distance, of at least several metres, separates the seat of the one from the offices of the other.

Apart from proximity, which here as elsewhere is a source of friction, the causes of the bad blood are various. First, there is the tactlessness or inexperience of many travellers who go to the head receptionist for their keys or to the concierge for their bills. But these are minor irritations within a dark and cloudy dispute. Among the possible explanations of such frequent incompatibility, the most disinterested observers have cited a difference of condition. The young men in the reception service, all graduates of the best hotel schools, thus bristling with knowledge and diplomas, full of aspiration towards the top, but salaried at a decent though modest rate, cast hostile eyes upon that somewhat insolent, just-watch-me person who takes his part of the 18 or 21 percent service charge, and then receives, for whatever answer he might give, tips substantial enough to double, triple, or quadruple his official income. On the other side, the concierge, even though the linchpin of the operation, the individual without whom nothing could go right, never forgets that he must wear livery, unlike the young, almost always snobbish and disdainful receptionists.

Formerly, receptionists devoted most of their time to handling the mail. In those days, all clients wrote to reserve their rooms long in advance, and the hotel had to carry on a veritable correspondence in order to assuage their anxieties or satisfy their various wishes — that is, take account of their second thoughts, beginning with the ritual of altered dates.

The telex and its never-ending snake of paper have greatly modified the life of the reception service. The computer already reigns in some grand hotels, which must adapt to its methods and reasonings. Moreover, one can imagine that the machine will one day answer, when queried about the future of palace hotels, that they are condemned to disappear, given their status as the last symbols of a past never to be recovered.

But, in the final count, poetry may prevail over the computer and its electronic cousins. The last grand European hotels have proved quite resistant to the imperatives of cost control and profitability. For a businessman, a banker, a corporation lawyer, however, palace hotels are the absolute paradigm of what should no longer be built or developed. But lo ! behind the décor, instead of renunciation, an attack is underway, and with the complicity of the financial groups upon which the hotel people depend, or of the president who encourages them to continue, and even sweeten, the venture. The directors, truly courageous leaders, ally reason and extravagance to protect what I am not too far wrong in calling their fabulous operas.

Recently, I met several of these key men, who however keep none of the golden keys that went with the livery once worn by their kind. Thanks to this ambiguity, they made quite an impression on me. Going and coming, like old-fashioned ambassadors, on a stage where an appearance by the Guermantes would hardly take them unawares, the new "management" move directly into the wings, and immediately proceed to change both their manner and their vocabulary. An instant later we must follow them through the most formidable work sites, whose hoardings they continually open, quite stealthily, behind the looking glass, so as to make their palace invulnerable, as was once done in Venice behind those sublime façades along the Grand Canal. What contemptible man, having heard that time and tide efface all, would give up writing or drawing in sand ? !

Looking glass, I said ! Alice did not go through it just to look. The objective was to look while being looked at. And there we are again ! Two different societies taking a peek at one another. At first sight, they are not on the same level, since one is at the service of the other, but the gentle servant enjoys a certain superiority by virtue of the fact that she passes in and out of both worlds. Alice, or Ariadne, or the author seeks a key, providing it does not come with a lock.

They would return from their search empty-handed, so said the maître at a famous palace, without however insisting on it, since the information seemed totally devoid of interest.

« You know, most of the servants here have been infected with a strange disease : mimesis. A past, a décor, a certain luxury are required. Naturally, the clientele no longer generates the same fascination of yore ; money and power are no longer in the same hands. But palaces have an effect on travellers ; they make them more attractive. Thus, many valets, hall porters, and chambermaids imitate them : their voices, their way of walking, of dressing, laughing, or wearing makeup. This desire for resemblance is usually without consequence or change of role. But sometimes the consequences are happy. By observing the manner of a great English photographer, for example, a footman has become a photographer in his own right, even one of the most famous. It seems possible that one day a servant, through mimesis, will take himself for a King or a Texas millionaire. Then the dream will have made a sharp — and wrong — turn.

At the beginning, I mentioned that dual desire which brings two societies to interface with one another, and the same taboo that keeps them apart. There are, however, certain short cuts through which either side can slip away — the looking glass, for example.

*Following pages:*
*on the left: concert hall*
*in the* Hotel Pupp, *Karlsbad;*
*on the right:*
*programme cover*
*for a Paris Show.*

175

# ACT II
# A NEW SCENE,
# A NEW SET

206

207

208

209

204 - *The hall of the* Hotel Colombia, Genoa// *At the end of the 1920's, Genoa still lacked an establishment which could meet the requirements of international tourism. Although the client were also seeking picturesque local color, they were freshly disembarked from sumptuous liners and they expected their stay in Genoa to come up to high standards of luxury and comfort. And so the* Hotel Colombia *came into existence. It was inaugurated on the 20th of February 1929, and the orchestra from the* Hotel Excelsior *in Rome was hired for the occasion. The cost of this inauguration illustrates the kind of image that the management of the new hotel sought to impose: 2,727 lire, of which 1,000 went for the musicians.*

205 and 208 - *The* Hotel Gellert, Budapest: *the swimming pool and the hotel (the last building on the right) in the row of façades along the Danube// The building of this hotel, inaugurated in 1918, was in keeping with a longstanding Budapest tradition. The city had been, from time immemorial, a place where visitors came to take the waters and spand their leisure time. The year after it opened, the* Gellert *became the scene of a tumultuous series of historic events. In March 1919, the government of the Hungarian Republic, under Bela Kun, moved into the* Gellert. *It was driven out in August by the occupying Rumanian army which set up its headquarters in the hotel. In November, the scenery shifted: up until April 1920 the hotel was the headquarters of the counter-revolutionary troops fighting Bela Kun and led by Admiral Horthy. However, despite its somewhat turbulent beginnings, the* Gellert *seems to have carried on with its normal activities since, in 1921, it was selected to be host for the International Hoteliers' Congress. In 1926, a fifthh floor was added on to the hotel.*

206 and 207 - *The* Palasthotel Quellenhorf *and its hydropathic baths, Aixla-Chapelle.*

209 - *Private dining room in the* Parkhotel, Frankfurt, *built in 1905.*

210 and 211 - *"Exotic" bedroom and fancy-dress ball at* Claridge's, London, *c. 1920.*

213

215

214

216

217

218

186

Interiors of Claridge's annex, designed in 1930-31 by the architect Oswald Milne: 212 - Corridor. 213 - Hexagonal vestibule leading to the Reception Hall. 214 - Drawing room of suite nº 102. 215 - Main corridor. 216 - Reception Hall // Claridge's was opened in 1812 by a Frenchman, called Mivart, whose excellent cuisine soon made the hotel's reputation. The "Morning Post" of 1827 described it as "the fashionable rendezvous for grand dignitaries of the diplomatic corps". In 1838 the hotel was acquired by William Claridge, a former maître d'hôtel. The new owner gave the establishment his own name but took care, for some years afterwards, to add "late Mivart's" so as to benefit from the reputation of the former business. Queen Victoria visited the Empress Eugénie at Claridge's when she was staying there in 1860. The Queen's enthusiasm for the hotel, immediately taken up by her entourage, soon justified Claridge's being known as "the Buckingham Palace annex". Bought in 1894 by Richard D'Oyle Carte, who had already created the Savoy, the hotel was rebuilt to meet the demand for new standards of comfort. Claridge's reopened in 1898 for the benefit of the very aristocratic clientele it has traditionally continued to serve. When Princess Elizabeth married Philip Mountbatten in 1947, there were so many royal guests at Claridge's that a diplomat, asking to speak to the King, received by way of reply: "Yes, but which one?"
217 and 218 - The French delegation at the Hotel Savoia Majestic and carabinieri on guard at the entrance to the Imperial Palace during the 1922 Geneva Conference. 219 - The 5th December 1923 election results posted up at the Savoy, London.

219

14·11·1922

*Norma Talmadge*     *Constance Talmadge*

# Savoy Hotel
### Tuesday November 14th
### 1922

*Margaret Leahy*

### Associated First National Pictures Ltd

### Banquet
to the Misses
## Norma and Constance
## Talmadge
and Mr. Joseph M. Schenck.

221

**Valentino** Mr & Mrs Rudolph

6776 Wedgwood Place
Los Angeles
Imp. Koller 14, r. Favart

| SÉJOURS | | APPT | PRIX | Maît. | Enf. | Gouv | Dom. | Pens. Dom. | OBSERVATIONS |
|---|---|---|---|---|---|---|---|---|---|
| ARRIVÉES | DÉPARTS | | | | | | | | |
| 15 Août 23 | 2 Sept.re 23 | 220-21 | 300 | 2 | | | | | |
| 26 Sept. 23 | 3 Octobre | 509.10 | 125 | 1 | | | | | |
| 27 Sept. 23 | 1923 | 654 | 40 | | | | | | Délogement |
| 18 Oct. 23 | 26 Oct. 23 | 233 | 125 | 2 | | | | | |
| 14 Déc 23 | 22 Déc | 204.05 | 300 | 1 | | | | | |
| 21 Déc 23 | 1923 | 204.05 | 300 | 2 | | | | | Arr: de Mme Valentino |
| 3 Janv. 24 | 5 Janv. 24 | 220.21 | 250 | 2 | | | | | |
| 19 Oct. 1924 | 24 Nov | 220.21.22 | 700 | 3 | | | | | avec Mr Richard Hudnut |
| 27 Oct 1924 | 1924 | 220.21 | 475 | 2 | | | | | Départ de d° d° |
| 27 Nov 1925 | 2 Déc 25 | 209.10 | 500 | 2 | | | | | avec son secrétaire Mr S.M. Reach |
| 13 Déc 1925 | 20 Déc 25 | 204.5.6 | 500 | 2 | | | | | d° d° |
| 27 Déc 1925 | 29 Déc 25 | 204.5.6 | 500 | 2 | | | | | d° d° |

20     222

223

224

225

226

220 - *The menu at the* Savoy Hotel, *London.*
221 - *Bibi in the restaurant of the* Grand Hôtel du Cap, *Antibes. Photo by Jacques-Henri Lartigue // The "Villa Soleil", originally a convalescent home for writers and artists, was converted into a hotel – the* Grand Hôtel du Cap *– in 1863. But almost straight away the Franco-Prussian war stopped it running as such. It was not until 1914 and the building of an annexe – the "Eden Roc" – that the hotel became a real millionaires' paradise, the "Hotel des Etrangers" that Scott Fitzgerald writes of in "Tender is the Night": "On the pleasant shore of the French Riviera, half way between Marseilles and the Italian border, stands a large, proud, rose-coloured hotel. Deferential palms cool its flushed façade and before it stretches a sharp dazzling beach. Lately it has become a summer resort of notable and fashionable people."*
222 - *"Cardex" of the* Plaza Athénée, *Paris, in the name of Mr. and Mrs. Rudolph Valentino, who frequently stayed at this hotel up to the year before the star's death // The "Cardex" was the sure guarantee of the exceptional service offered by the "Palaces". All particulars were carefully noted down and kept up to date: the guest's name, private address, the dates of successive visits, choice of suite, amount spent, the staff detailed to look after him, etc. This "aide-mémoire" meant that a guest could be made to feel personally welcome and expected at all times, however many or diverse the clientele.*
223 - *Mrs. Beamish, the King of Sweden, Miss Lenglen and the ex-King of Portugal on one of the seven tennis courts of the* Hôtel Beau Site, *Cannes // It was in the park of this hotel that the Renshaw brothers built the first hard courts and that French tennis was born.*
224 - *The beach of the* Lido, *Venice.*
225 - *The Floral Festival, Monte-Carlo, in front of the* Hôtel de Paris, *in 1919.*
226 - *Politicians at the* Palace Hotel, *Bussaco, 1926.*

# L'Eclaireur du Dimanche

## MONDAIN THÉATRAL SPORTIF

Mlle Grace OVIDE, la jolie danseuse du Ruhl

*Liste Officielle des Etrangers*

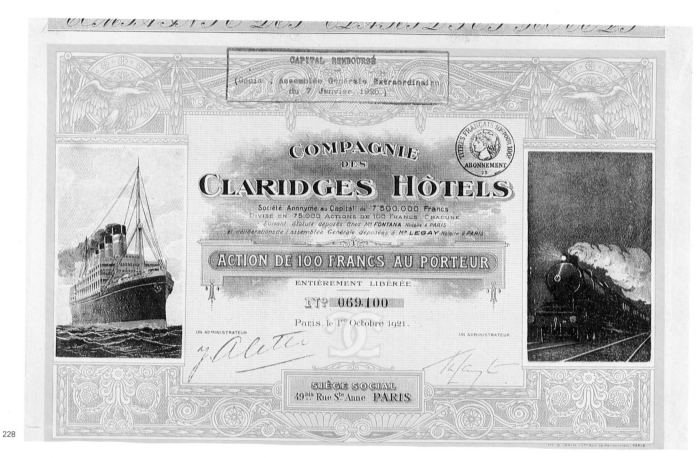

228

229

196

232

231

233

227 - The "Eclaireur du dimanche", a Riviera society
paper which published,
among other items, a daily
updated list of residents in
the local hotels.
228 - A share certificate for
the Hôtel Claridge, Paris.
229 - The Hotel Europa,
Heidelburg: luggage label//
This hotel, built in 1865,
was extensively redeveloped
in the thrities.
230 - Ice decor and operetta
airship for a party, in 1927,
with a "North Pole" theme
at the Hotel Excelsior,
Lido, Venice.
231 and 233 - "La Verbena
del Amor", in 1928, was
one of the biggest parties
held in the Hôtel du Pa-
lais, Biarritz.
232 - The first act of
"l'Ecole des Gigolos", performed in the Biarritz mu-
nicipal casino, tells of how
the gilded youth in their palaces enjoy evoking the demi-
monde: these boys and girls
are all from the very best
of French, German and
Spanish society.
234 - Serge Lifar, Diaghilev's favourite performer,
dancing at the Hotel des
Bains, Lido, Venice, the
very hotel in which the famous choreographer of the
"Ballets Russes" was to die
on August 19th, 1929// In
1980, Serge Lifar, then 75
years old, recalled: "Quar-
ter to six in the morning.
We're in the large bedroom
in the Hotel des Bains. I
see Diaghilev's head sud-
denly fall back. At that very
moment, the first beam of
sunlight is out over the sea.
Playing through the window
like the beam from a theatre
spotlight it falls on the tear,
the single tear slowly rolling
down Diaghilev's cheek. It
seems to me as if it were a
large glistening diamond
rather than a tear... Fifty
years later, this tear
is still sparkling ever
brighter."
235 - A party dedicated to
the mythical island of
Zanzibar, in 1924, at the
Hotel des Bains, Lido,
Venice.
236 - A fancy dress ball at
the Hôtel Négresco,
Nice.

234

198

235

236

199

237 and 239 - *Preparing for the New Year's Eve party, 1926, and Christmas party at the Savoy Hotel, London// The Savoy was renowned for its spectacular parties, some of which are remembered to this day. Such is the case of the Christmas dinner given by George A. Kessler, the champagne magnate, in honor of Perry, the American explorer who reached the North Pole in 1909. The evening festivities took place in the Palm Court: the floor was completely carpeted with artificial snow and the walls festooned with masses of enormous white chrysanthemums. The menu was presented on a gigantic nail symbolizing the Pole. It included, among other delicacies, "Siberian caviar", "North Pole Perigord truffles" and an "Eskimo ice pudding". Little snowmen, each inscribed with a name, guided the guests to their assigned seats at the dinner table and each of the ladies was offered a bouquet of white gardenias. Kessler had 400 presents (for 34 guests!) brought over from Paris — among the presents were gold Cartier cigarette cases for the men and diamond brooches from the Rue de Rivoli for the ladies...*
238 - *Christmas decorations at* Claridge's, London.

238

239

201

240

241                                                    24

202

243

244

245

246    247

207

248

249

250

251

252

254

255

211

256

257

260

261

262
263

256 - *The* Hôtel du Golf, *Deauville : luggage label. This hotel was built in 1925.*

257 - *"Tea time in Chiberta: throughout the winter, the links are crowded with players, charmed by the beautiful course; here we can see, together in the clubhouse, the Count and Countess F. de Chevigné, Mr. and Mrs. A. de Aguilar,*
*Misses de Amezaga, Mr. and Mrs. da Silva Ramos and Mr. Roy Mac Williams (from a society column,*
*Biarritz, 1935).*

258 - *The* Grand Hôtel de l'Ermitage, *Vittel, built in 1929. Behind what might look like an ordinary Swiss hotel, built of pink sandstone, ochre stone and polychromatic ceramics, is an ultra-modern palace. In the foreground, the golf-course laid out on former marshland.*

259 - *The* Royal Hôtel, *Evian (1901-1909)// From a thirties publicity brochure with its heady lyricism :*
*"The* Royal *commands an incomparable view over the blue waters of Lake Leman. From its flower festooned terrasse each hour ushers in new enchantment. Now the morning sun casts a mantle of light mist on the quilted backdrop of the lake, now its sparkling waters blaze under the midday star, now the silvery waves are bathed in the gold of sundown."*

260 - *The entrance of the* Hôtel de Crillon, *Paris.*

261 - *Client and porter at the* Hôtel George V, *Paris.*

262 - *Mistinguett arriving at the* Hôtel Martinez, *Cannes, in 1938.*

263 - *Churchill and Lloyd George leaving the* Hôtel Carlton, *Cannes, in 1938. They were both there for the banquet given by Churchill to celebrate the golden wedding anniversary of Mr. and Mrs. Lloyd George.*

264

265

216

266

267

268

269

270

271

219

273

274

N. 1417          Lido di Venezia          Il the nel giardino dell' Excelsior Palace Hotel

264 - *Winter Palace hotel, Menton: the winter garden.*

265 - *Dining- room of the* Hôtel du Beach, *Monte Carlo, built in 1928.*

266 - Hôtel Martinez, *Cannes: the façade // The Côte d'Azur's tourist history was to take a decisive turn at the beginning of the 1930's with the advent of the "Summer Season" and the appearance of a new summer holiday clientele. A remarkable hotel-boom ensued. It was in this context that the* Hotel Martinez, *a eight-storey building of 600 bedrooms and drawing rooms, opened in 1929. The old-established mediterranean palace-hotels benefited similarly from this new passion for sun-bathing. Thus the Cannes* Carlton, *in such difficulties at the end of the war that in 1919 it had been put on the market for 1 million francs, was to recover its past affluence in the August of 1930. That year it had rained so heavily everywhere, except of course on the Côte d'Azur, that the management, taking a risk, decided to open the hotel which until then had closed during the summer. The sequel proved the soundness of their judgement.*

267 - *The* Grand Hôtel, *Vittel: the Pavillon de Cérès restaurant, renovated in 1936 by Fernand César.*

268 and 270 - Hôtel du Beach, *Monte Carlo: a pedalo in front of the hotel's beach and lazing on the terrace.*

269 - Grand Hotel des Bains, *the Lido, Venice: the Viennese actrice, M. Weiss, on the beach.*

271 - *A meeting in front of the* Hôtel du Palais d'Orsay, *Paris (from the film "The Conformist" by B. Bertolucci).*

272 and 273 - Hôtel des Ambassadeurs, *Rome, built in 1927: a fresco and the façade.*

274 - Hôtel Excelsior, *the Lido, Venice: a "thé dansant" in the gardens.*

HOTEL
MAJESTIC
CANNES

276

277

223

279

280

275 - *The American Bar in the* Grand Hôtel, *Paris.*
276 - *The main entrance of the* Savoy Hotel: *the private entrance, for the sole use of guests' cars, is the only place in England where one drives on the right.*
277 - *The bar-restaurant and cinema in the* Grand Etablissement des Bains, *Lido, Venice.*
278 - *A reception in the* Hôtel Meurice, *Paris – Dresses by Jeanne Lanvin (1930).*
279 - *Reception in the* Hôtel de Paris, *Monte Carlo (1930).*
280 - *Ballroom in the* Dorchester Hotel, *London.*
281 - *Jazz at the* Savoy Hotel, *London.// During the twenties American rhythm swept over Europe. It was at this time that the Savoy's manager, George Reeves-Smith – a great jazz fan – hired Bert Ralton and his Havana Band so that the guests could dance each evening. The move met such an enthusiastic reception that a second band, Debroy Somers', was taken on. They were to become the celebrated "Savoy Orpheans". The band soon became world famous as, from 1923, the young BBC began to broadcast evening entertainment from the Savoy. Each night all England would tune into "Dance Music from the Savoy" on the wireless, and down at Cowes couples would dance in the moonlight on their yachts to the "Missouri Waltz", "Three o'clock in the morning" or "Valencia". The programme could be heard as far away as Long Island. Marconi told the story of a French batallion in North Africa, besieged by the enemy, who managed to pick up the Savoy programme and all the soldiers who weren't on guard duty danced their cares away. They danced so much and so well that a daily half hour truce was observed so that the two armies might enjoy their favorite music undisturbed. The "Savoy Orpheans" gave the first performance of "Rhapsody in Blue", with George Gershwin himself playing piano.*
282 - *"Fête nègre" at the* Palm Beach, *Cannes ; the casino was built in 1928.*
283 - *Dinner in the* Hôtel Carlton, *Cannes.*
284 - *The Monte Carlo Casino.*

281

282

226

283

284

285

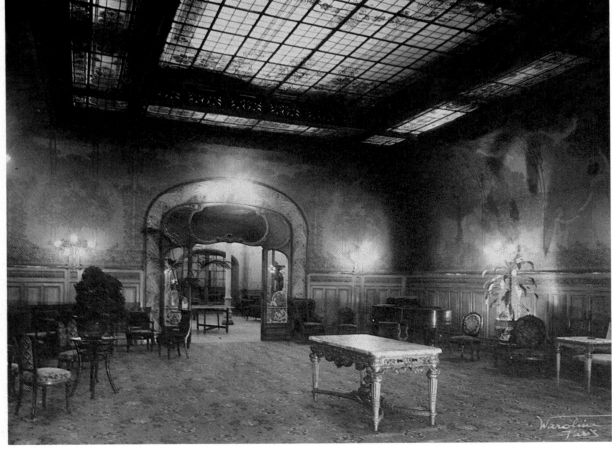

286

287

288

289

290

291

292

285 - *The reading room in the* Hôtel Regina, *Paris. During the last World War, when the hotel was requisitioned by the occupying forces, this room was turned into a table tennis room for German officers.* 286 - *The dining- room.*

287 - *The bar in the* Hôtel Plaza Athénée *in the 1940's// It was in this bar that Mata Hari, accused of being a German spy, was arrested before being shot in 1917. The celebrated adventuress would often stay at the Plaza Athénée, in room 120 looking out onto the garden. However, the day she was arrested, she had only dropped into the hotel, as she was at that time staying at the* Elysée Palace Hôtel.

288 - *It was in this dining room in the* Hôtel Raphaël, *Paris, that Hitler is said to have dined with General Stumnagel and his staff.*

289 - *Field Marshal Pétain leaving the* Thermal Palace, Vichy.

290 and 291 - *The* Dorchester Hotel, London, *1940: the entrance protected by sandbags and the staff posing with members of the Fire bomb squad// During the war, the* Dorchester *lost a lot of its staff and its habitual clientele and underwent the rigors of the black-out and rationing. However, it was never empty. Indeed, as it was built in reinforced concrete, it was considered one of the safest places to be during the bombing. And so, many Londoners, including several members of the government, put up here. When there was an alert, they found shelter in the Turkish baths, in the kitchens, the very bravest in their beds which had been installed in the corridors.*

292 - *Staff on strike, in 1946, at the* Savoy Hotel, London.

294

295

233

296

297

298

299

300

301

302

303

304

305

306

307

308

30

310

311

240

312

307 - *The entrance of the* Hotel Ritz, *Madrid.*
308 and 309 - *Field Marshal Montgomery leaving* Claridge's, *London, and Miss Jane Rotinoff setting off for the Adelphi Theatre where she is to take part in a grand charity reception given by Miss Violet Ballantine.*
310 - *The American bar in the* Hôtel de Crillon, *Paris.*
311 and 312 - *The* Hôtel Claridge, *Paris: bar and dance-floor.*
313 - *Dinner dance at the* Hôtel Quirinale, *Rome.* // *"There were five people at the Quirinale bar after dinner. An Italian woman perched on a bar-stool, who insisted on chatting to the barman whose only reply was "si... si... si...", a snobbish young Egyptian who looked rather lonely but was wary of the woman and the two Americans". (Scott Fitzgerald – "Tender is the night")*

Hotel Atlantic, *Hamburg*
Hotel Grande Bretagne, *Athens.*

313

241

317

318

319

320

314 - *Sophia Loren in Cannes.* // *The idea of an international film festival dates from 1938. It was intended to counterbalance the La Mostra festival in Venice, too pro-German and pro-Italian. Two towns were candidates: Biarritz and Cannes, and finally it was Cannes that won the day. The first festival was to open on September 1st. 1939; the Second World War postponed everything until September 20th. 1946. From then on, the Carlton beach became the favoured spot for starlets and producers and the hotels were filled with an eclectic and extravagant clientele.*

315 - *The boot-black at the* Hôtel Claridge, *Paris.*

316 - *Charlie Chaplin and his wife on the roof of the* Savoy Hotel, *London.*

317 - *Judy Garland filling out her Census form with the help of the manager of the* Dorchester Hotel, *London, 1951.*

318 - *Edward G. Robinson at the* Hotel Danieli, *Venice.*

319 - *Anna Magnani in front of the* Hotel Excelsior, *Naples.*

320 - *Katharine Hepburn at* Claridge's, *London.*

321 - *Prince Rainier and Princess Grace of Monaco at the* Hotel Colombia, *Genoa.*

322 - *Queen Elizabeth at the* Hyde Park Hotel, *London.*

323 - *Salvador Dali at the* Hôtel Meurice, *Paris, where he was a regular guest. Standing in front of his painting, Dali is explaining the art of tunny fishing to the staff.* // *The annals of the hotel are full of tales of his excentric behavior. For example it was required etiquette to toss twenty centime coins under the wheels of his car, each time the master, "rolling in money", left the hotel.*

324 - *Marilyn Monroe in 1956, accompanied by Sir Laurence Olivier and Arthur Miller, at a press conference held in the* Savoy Hotel, *London, for the launching of the film "The Sleeping Prince".*

321

322

246

323

324

325

326

327

328

329

250

330

251

333

334

Les Derniers seront
les premiers!
Sarah Bernhardt
1914

Leaves From an Album

337

Bruxelles. Hôtel Métropole et la Place de Brouckère.

338

13 VITTEL. — Escalier de l'Hôtel de l'Etablissement. — LL.

339

340

341

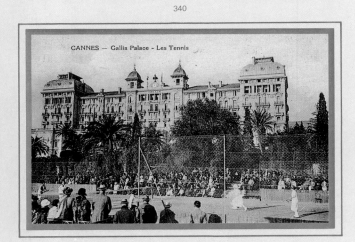

CANNES — Gallia Palace - Les Tennis

342

50 — NICE - CIMIEZ    Riviera-Palace - Hôtel

343

115 LA BAULE - Hôtel l'Hermitage

344

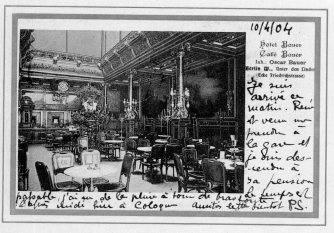

Hotel Bauer
Café Bauer
Inh.: Oscar Bauer
Berlin W., Unter den Linden
(Ecke Friedrichstrasse)

345

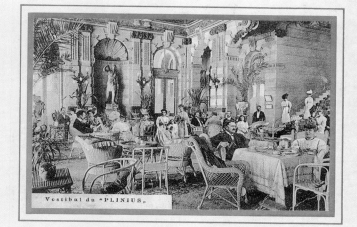

Vestibul du „PLINIUS"

346

88 CABOURG: — Le Grand Hôtel. — LL.

347

HOTEL RAPHAEL, 17, AVENUE KLEBER, PARIS

348

Spiaggia di Rimini - La piattaforma con vista del Grand Hôtel

349

350

PARIS. GRAND-HOTEL. — Restaurant.

351

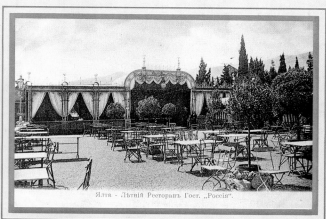

Ялта - Лѣтній Ресторанъ Гост. „Россія".

352

HÔTEL NEGRESCO, NICE
37, PROMENADE DES ANGLAIS

353

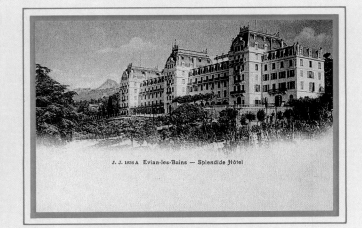

J. J. 1886 A  Evian-les-Bains — Splendide Hôtel

354

355

72.  DEAUVILLE — Le " Normandy Hôtel " et la rue Gontaut-Biron

356

BIARRITZ
Rendez-vous de Chasse au Grand-Hôtel - 1er Mars 1909

357

358

359

360

361

362

363

364

365

366

367

368

3. CANNES — L'Esplanade des Alliés et les Hôtels

369

370

G. M. 1365. Dieppe. — Les Hôtels vus du Boulevard

371

1310 Dieppe. — Régina Palace Hôtel

372

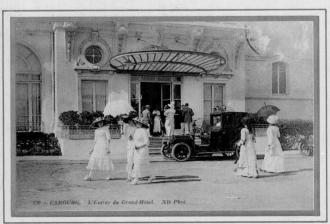

Rimini — Il Grand Hôtel e la Spiaggia

373

Côte d'Azur    57    NICE — Hôtel Ruhl - Ruhl Hotel

374

129 — CABOURG. L'Entrée du Grand-Hôtel. ND Phot.

375

25. — Le Touquet-Paris-Plage. — L'Hermitage

376

377

J. J. 7512 be Caux-Palace en hiver

378

379

380

Bucureştï.
Hotel Bristol. — Bulevardul Elisabeta.

381

382

Royal Palace Hôtel
Ostende    14 Mai 1902

383

384

Bagnoles-de-l'Orne. - Le Grand Hôtel de l'Établissement Thermal

385

386

387

388

LE LORD-MAIRE A PARIS, 15 OCTOBRE 1906
Le Carrosse du Lord-Maire au Grand-Hôtel

389

Genova - Piazza Acquaverde e Monumento a C. Colombo

390

4248. PARIS - Gare d'Orsay
Construite en 1900, Architecte Laloux

391

392

393

394

395

396

397

398

399

400

9 — PARIS - Hôtel du Louvre - Intérieur de la Salle à Manger

401

Caves et Comestibles du Terminus-Hôtel — Gare Saint-Lazare - Paris

402

Paris - Grand-Hôtel - Le Jardin d'hiver

403

8 — PARIS - Cour du Grand Hôtel du Louvre

404

Paris. - Hôtel Continental. - Le Salon Mauresque

405

406

407

408

409

410

Вологда. Гостиница и ресторанъ
„Золотой Якорь".
2-е изданіе.

Vologe
Hôtel de l'Ancre d'

411

412

„Pupp's Parkhaus".

Karlsbad.

413

„Hotel Caraiman"

Sinaia

414

HÔTEL IMPERIAL

415

416

336 - *The lift in the* Hôtel Meurice, *Paris.*
337 - *The* Grand Hôtel Pupp, *Carlsbad.*
338 - *The* Hôtel Métropole, *Brussels.*
339 - *The* Grand Hôtel de l'Établissement, *Vittel.*
340 - *The* Hôtel Majestic, *Vichy.*
341 - *The* Grand Hôtel Boulevard, *Bucharest.*
342 - *The* Hôtel Gallia, *Cannes: the tennis courts.*
343 - *The* Riviera Palace Hôtel, *Nice.*
344 - *The* Hôtel Hermitage, *La Baule.*
345 - *The* Hotel Bauer, *Berlin.*
346 - *The* Grand Hôtel Plinius, *Lake Como.*
347 - *The* Grand Hôtel, *Cabourg.*
348 - *The* Hôtel Raphaël, *Paris.*
349 - *The* Grand Hôtel, *Rimini.*
350 - *The* Langham Hotel, *London.*
351 - *The* Grand Hôtel, *Paris.*
352 - *The* Hôtel de Russie, *Yalta.*
353 - *The* Hôtel Négresco, *Nice.*
354 - *The* Hôtel Splendide, *Évian-les-Bains.*
355 - *The* Hôtel Eskualduna, *Hendaye.*
356 - *The* Hôtel Normandy, *Deauville.*
357 - *The* Grand Hôtel, *Biarritz: a meet before a hunt.*
358 - *The* Palace Hotel, *Madrid.*
359 - *The* Majestic Palace, *Nice.*
360 - *The* Grand Hôtel, *Nancy.*
361 - *The* Grand Hôtel de l'Europe, *Saint Petersburg.*
362 - *The* Grand Hôtel du Parc, *Vichy.*
363 - *The* Piccadilly Hotel, *London: the restaurant.*
364 - *The* Hôtel Splendide, *Évian-les-Bains.*
365 - *The* Hôtel Majestic, *Cannes.*
366 - *The* Hôtel Regina, *Biarritz.*
367 - *The* Hôtel Regina, *Saint Petersburg.*
368 - *The* Midland Hotel, *Manchester.*
369 - *The* Esplanade des Alliés *and the hotels., Cannes.*
370 - *The* Hôtel Royal, *Deauville.*
371 - *The* hotels seen from the esplanade, *Dieppe.*
372 - *The* Regina Palace Hôtel, *Dieppe.*
373 - *The* Grand Hôtel, *Rimini.*
374 - *The* Hôtel Ruhl, *Nice.*
375 - *The* Grand Hôtel, *Cabourg: entrance.*
376 - *The* Hôtel Hermitage, *Le Touquet Paris-Plage.*
377 - *The* Grand Hôtel, *Houlgate.*
378 - *The* Caux Palace Hôtel, *Caux, in winter.*
379 - *The* Hôtel Royal Picardy, *Le Touquet Paris-Plage.*
380 - *The* Richmond Hotel, *London.*
381 - *The* Hotel Bristol, *Bucharest.*
382 - *The* Hôtel d'Angleterre, *Copenhagen.*
383 - *The* Royal Palace Hotel, *Ostend.*
384 - *The* Grand Hôtel, *Bellagio.*
385 - *The* Grand Hôtel de l'Établissement Thermal, *Bagnoles-de-l'Orne.*
386 - *The* Brenner's Park Hotel annex, *Baden-Baden.*
387 - *The* Grand Hôtel, *Bellagio.*
388 - *The* Hôtel Maria Christina, *San Sebastian.*
389 - *The* Lord Mayor of London at the *Grand Hôtel, Paris, 1906.*
390 - *The* Grand Hôtel Savoia, *Genoa.*
391 - *the station and the* Hôtel du Palais d'Orsay, *Paris.*
392 - *The* Hôtel Continental, *Milan: the bar.*
393 - *The* Hotel Astoria, *Coimbra.*
394 - *The* Dom Hotel, *Cologne.*
395 - *The* Hôtel Excelsior, *Lido, Venice: the kitchens.*
396 - *The* Grand Hôtel National, *Lucerne.*
397 - *The* Hôtel Reine Victoria, *Palma de Mallorca.*
398 - *The* Vittel Palace *and the* Grand Hôtel, *Vittel.*
399 - *The* Hôtel Mirabeau, *Aix-les-Bains.*
400 - *The* Grand Hôtel du Parc *and the* Hôtel des Princes, *Châtelguyon.*
401 - *The* Grand Hôtel du Louvre, *Paris: the dining room.*
402 - *The* Hôtel Terminus, *Saint-Lazare Station, Paris.*
403 - *The* Palm Court of the *Grand Hôtel, Paris.*
404 - *The* Grand Hôtel du Louvre, *Paris: the courtyard.*
405 - *The* Hôtel Continental, *Paris: the Moorish saloon.*
406 - *The* Hotel Europäischerhof, *Baden-Baden.*
407 - *The* Turin Palace Hotel, *Turin.*
408 - *The* Hôtel des Trois Couronnes, *Vevey.*
409 - *The* Grand Hôtel, *Stockholm.*
410 - *The* Grand Hôtel, *Stary Smokovec.*
411 - *The* Hôtel de l'Ancre d'Or, *Valogda.*
412 - *The* Grand Hôtel Victoria - Jungfrau, *Interlaken.*
413 - *The* Grand Hôtel Pupp, *Karlsbad.*
414 - *The* Hotel Caraiman, *Sinaio.*
415 - *The* Hôtel Imperial, *Vienna (before alteration).*
416 - *The* Hôtel Imperial, *Vienna (with a new floor added on).*

# INDEX

This index covers european hotels that came into being between 1800 and 1930, and those whose final form was established or reconstructed during that period.

*Front cover*:
Hôtel de Crillon, Paris: *the dining room*.
*Photographer: J.N. de Soye*.
*Back cover*:
Impérial Palace Hôtel, *Annecy*.

ALETTI: 340, 362. ARCHIVES ARCHITECTURE MODERNE (BRUXELLES): 65, 66, 151. ASSOCIATION LARTIGUE: 221. BIASINI: 87. BIBLIOTHEQUE DE L'ARSENAL (PARIS): 183. BIBLIOTHEQUE DE VERSAILLES: 59. BIBLIOTHEQUE HISTORIQUE DE LA VILLE DE PARIS: 55, 68, 69, 70, 107, 177, 246, 391. BIBLIOTHEQUE NATIONALE (PARIS): 341, 370, 376, 381, 398, 414. BOHM: 162. BOISSEL: 351, 365, 369, 376, 389, 401, 404, 405. CAHIERS DU CINEMA: 271. CARLE: 83, 222, 228, 231, 232, 251, 257, 262, 263, 283, 337, 342, 343, 347, 350, 356, 357, 363, 366, 371, 372, 375, 377, 396, 402. COMPAGNIE INTERNATIONALE DES WAGONS-LITS ET DU TOURISME: *p. 7*, 60, 61. DE BUISSON: *p. 153*, 244, 354, 364. FOUREAU: 256. GALLIA: 346. GAUTHIER: *p. 177*, 345, 367, 378. GIRARDEL: 176, 258. GIRAUDON: 81, *p. 154*. INSTITUT FRANÇAIS D'ARCHITECTURE (PARIS): 73, 78, 267. KEYSTONE (LONDON): 292, 295, 308, 309, 316, 320, 324. KEYSTONE (PARIS): 99, 100, 124, 248, 249, 250, 252, 261, 287. KRAINICK NEGRESCO: 189, 353. MAGNUM: 329, 330. MUSEE DE L'AFFICHE (PARIS): 89. MUSEE DES ARTS DECORATIFS (PARIS): 5, 6, 7, 86, 88, 101, 102, 104, 105, 108, 109, 110, 111, 112, 114, 115, 125, 126, 135, 136, 137, 138, 146, 147, 153, 171, 172, 179, 355, 358, 359. MUSEE DES DEUX GUERRES MONDIALES (PARIS): 191, 192. NATIONAL MONUMENTS RECORD (LONDON): *p. 2, 3, p. 14*, 8, 25, 32, 52, 74, 75, 93, 140, 141, 144, 154, 165, 166, 167, 168, 174, 175, 190, 203, 242. NIERMANS: 91, 106, 118, 119, 120, 121. PARIS-MATCH: 314, 328. PLOUSEAU: 311, 312, 334. PRESSES-SPORT: 196. PYLIAVSKY: 149. ROGER VIOLLET: *p. 21, p. 22*, 3, 4, 28, 31, 33, 34, 35, 50, 51, 57, 58, 62, *p. 172*, 259, 289, 403. SAVINE: 352, 361, 411. SIROT: 30, 85, 103, 339, 383, 399, 413. SOCIETE DES BAINS DE MER (MONTE CARLO): 82, 225, 265, 268, 270, 279, 284. SPADEM: *p. 26*, 123, 145, 159, 160, *p. 164*, 253, 260, 294, 301, 310, 315. THE BETTMANN ARCHIVE (NEW YORK): *p. 12*. WEIL: 344, 368, 378, 379, 380, 385, 397, 400.

─────────── PHOTOGRAPHERS ───────────
BOUCHART (FRANÇOIS XAVIER): 26, 36, 37, 71, 173, *p. 146*, 264, 266. ENRIETTI: 91. FELTON: 212, 242. FREED (LEONARD): 330. GIACOMELLI: 234. HERTZ: 267. LACROIX (MARC): 76, 326. LARTIGUE: 221. LEMERE (BEDFORD): *p. 2, 3*, 74, 75, 144, 166, 167, 168, 175, 203, 210, 211, 238. LE QUERREC: 329. NAVARO: 231, 233. NAYA: 120, 162. NEWTON (HELMUT): 332. PARKINSON (NORMAN): 305, 306. REY: 223. RISTELCHUBBER: 267. RUGGERI: 240. SALAUN: 68, 69, 70. SCARABELLO (GIOVANNI): 143, 224, 277. SCHALL (ROGER): *p. 9, p. 16, p. 147, p. 151, p. 173*, 296, 297, 298, 299, 300, 311, 312, 333. SEEBERGER: *p. 26*, 123, 145, 159, 160, *p. 164*, 253, 260, 301, 310, 315. SERGYSELS: 152. SIMON: 314. SOYE (JEAN NOEL DE): 56, 46, 325. THEVENARD (ARTHUR): 205.